TROUBLES and KUDDLES

A NOVEL

by

BERT GOOLSBY

Troubles and Kuddles

Copyright © 2016 and 2018 Bert Goolsby

This work may not be reproduced, transmitted, or stored in whole or in part by any means whatsoever without the express written consent of the author or his designee.
© 2016 Cover Art Work by Sue Husman
Original Cover Design © by Laura Shinn
Original Editing Copyright (2017) by Paula Martin
Original Executive Production by Karen Michelle Nutt

All rights reserved under U.S. and International copyright law. This Review and Promotions copy is licensed only for the private use of the reviewer or for the author to use as contest and promotional prizes. May not be copied, scanned, digitally reproduced, or printed for re-sale, may not be uploaded on shareware or free sites, or used in any other manner without the express written permission of the author and/or publisher. Thank you for respecting the hard work of the author.

Troubles and Kuddles is a work of fiction. Though actual locations may be mentioned, they are used in a fictitious manner and the events and occurrences were invented in the mind and imagination of the author except for the inclusion of actual historical facts. Similarities of characters or names used within to any person – past, present, or future – are coincidental except where actual historical characters are purposely interwoven.

Dedicated to my friend and former colleague Judge Jasper M. Cureton, a judge's judge

Other Works
by
Bert Goolsby

Fiction:

Purple Yarn
Finding Roda Anne
The Locusts of Padgett County
The Trials of Lawyer Pratt
Familiar Shadows
Five Stockings
Harpers' Joy
Her Own Law
Humanity, Darling
Sweet Potato Biscuits and
    Other Stories
The Box with the Green Bow
    And Ribbon
On Grandma' Porch (anthology
    with other authors)
More Sweet Tea (anthology
    with other authors)

Nonfiction:
His Wonders to Perform
Devotional Briefs
Lex Christi
90 Devotions for Lawyers & Judges
    and Those They Serve
The South Carolina Tort Claims Act:
    a Primer and Then Some

"It is a pleasant world we live in, sir, a very pleasant world. There are bad people in it, Mr. Richard, but if there were no bad people, there would be no good lawyers."
— Charles Dickens, *The Old Curiosity Shop*

CHAPTER ONE

Deloris Meek, dressed in his trademark double-breasted, now yellowish, used-to-be white suit, sat trembling at one of two counsel tables in the quiet of the main courtroom of the state court of appeals, a room fitted with black, Italian marble walls and reddish-brown mahogany millwork. An off-white, arched ceiling bordered by plaster details performed by hands long dead complemented a soothing, light-blue carpet beneath. The floor covering, however, did nothing to calm Deloris' jitters.

In anticipation of the court's entrance, a score or more of lawyers, litigants, and other interested parties entered through a single door at the rear of the courtroom and sauntered down a middle aisle before sidestepping into one of several bench rows. These pew-like fixtures, also of mahogany, sat behind a gated, brass railing that separated them from the well of the courtroom. The latter area held the lectern and two counsel tables with their chairs.

"Know what?" Deloris whispered to Billy Joe Pratt, a fellow lawyer who sat next to him, not as co-counsel but for moral support, "this place makes me feel like I don't even belong here—like the feeling I got my first day in algebra class. Makes me real nervous. You nervous?" Deloris crossed and uncrossed his legs and repeated the action seconds later.

Pratt ran his hand through his 70/30 side-parted black hair and laughed as he glanced toward the clerk of court, a bird-sized woman known for her efficiency as much as for her bad attitude. A woman of advanced years, she sat perched to Deloris' left several feet beyond the bench, a long, desk-like fixture designed for nine judges but more frequently used by three-judge panels. The clerk had not spoken to Deloris other than to ask his name, the party he represented, and how much time he required to argue his position.

"Why should I be nervous?" Billy Joe said. "This is your baby. I ain't got nothing in the world to do with it."

Deloris sucked in some air through closed teeth and brushed back his thinning red hair. "Man o' man, I wish I'd never gotten myself involved with this durn thing."

Pratt sat back in his chair and stared at Deloris. "Really? Handling this one makes a whole lot more sense to me than some of those other cases you've brought."

"Like what?"

"Like what? Like the wrongful-death action you brought for the man who choked to death on a pulley-bone at The Chicken Run. Remember that one? You claimed the pulley-bone represented a 'latent defect' which they should've warned the man about. Come on. It didn't take the judge two seconds to throw that case out and you with it. Every chicken's got a pulley bone, for heaven's sake."

"I still believe it was good case. I mean, how'd my man know the piece of chicken he was eating still had a pulley-bone in it. Don't everybody cut chicken up the same way, you know."

Deloris hunched forward, rubbing his hands between his legs and breathing hard.

Billy Joe patted Deloris on his shoulder. "Deloris, you gotta calm down."

"I can't. I'll tell you one thing, if I'd known it was gonna wind up like this—you know, me having to argue to the court of appeals—I'd've told Ginger to go get her somebody else to handle it. I've never argued an appeal before, and I don't mind telling you I'm about to mess in my britches. Somebody told me one time the judges here, they'll plumb jump the bench to get at you."

Deloris dropped his head and shook it. "Oh, me. Ever since I met that woman it seems like she and her former partner haven't offered me anything but trouble. Makes me wonder what's gonna happen next if I don't get shed of her."

The "Ginger" Deloris referred to was Ginger Childree, a former member of a ventriloquist act called "Wally and Ginger, Kody and Kuddles." He had met Ginger and her former partner Eli Fromberg, also known as Wally Teal, when they had hitchhiked a ride with him while he and Dixie St. John, a legal secretary who worked for Billy Joe, traveled to Texas in search of a missing heiress. The case before the court of appeals involved ownership of "Kuddles," a ventriloquist dummy Ginger had used in her and Fromberg's act.

Billy Joe elbowed Deloris' side. "Listen to you, talking about trouble. Don't you remember what Professor Karesh said about that?"

"No."

"He told us troubles and lawyers are two sides of the same coin, and it's the law that brings them both together and forms them into one."

"Your point?"

"Troubles are a lawyer's bread and butter, Deloris. You don't see that? The more troubles there are, the more work there is for lawyers. And the more work there is for the lawyers, the more money they'll make. Other words, troubles and lawyers go together like mayonnaise and tomatoes on light bread."

"Maybe so, but I can do without this kind, doncha know."

"You're getting yourself all worked up for nothing. Take a deep breath and try not to think about it for a moment. You'll do fine," Billy Joe said.

Deloris detected a note of uncertainty in Billy Joe's voice.

"Listen," Billy Joe continued, "all you gotta do is act like you do when you're talking to some of your buddies at the Rosewater Lounge. That's all there is to it."

"How would you know? You've never argued a case up here neither. I still don't know why you wanted to come with me anyway. You're not helping me a bit, you know."

Billy Joe put a hand to his mouth and leaned toward Deloris. He nodded toward the clerk. "Deloris, look there at that old woman. You think maybe she's got on a wig? Bet she does. Whatcha wanna bet? Might even be a bird nesting it. A turkey buzzard, maybe."

Before he could respond, Deloris heard someone say, "Morning, gentlemen." He turned toward the sound of the voice to see his opposition, Etheridge Morphie, III, of Morphie, Morphie, and Hatcher, Attorneys and Counselors at Law. He stood over Deloris and Billy Joe, his chin and nose uplifted as though the two of them emitted a foul odor. Deloris dipped his head and whispered back a good morning as the older lawyer set his brief case on the opposite counsel table and strode to the clerk of court's desk to register his appearance.

Afterward, Morphie returned to his table, saying to Deloris with a mocking laugh and pointing to Billy Joe as he walked past, "Pray tell, why did you bring Mr. Pratt along with you this morning? By any chance, is he Kuddles' daddy?"

Billy Joe leaned back in his chair and crossed his arms. "Yeah, that's right, I sure am. But her mama is a Morphie."

The old man's face reddened, and his mouth twitched. "Well, I'll say. I was only making a small joke, sir. You need not get so personal."

Billy Joe adjusted his black horn-rimmed glasses. "What? Me get personal?"

Deloris sensed Billy Joe rise from his chair and sit down again. He noticed the clerk, whom the practicing appellate bar called "Madam Meanness" behind her back, had directed pursed lips and narrowed eyes at Billy Joe. Rumor had it her look could cause diarrhea and even end pregnancies.

Minutes went by, rendering Deloris more nervous. His hands now shook. He tried putting them inside his pants pocket to stop their shaking, but to no avail. If anything, they made his leg start bouncing. He glanced over at Morphie. The old man sat straight in his chair, appearing composed and confident. He stared ahead, his hands joined together as they rested on the table, neither note nor legal pad in front of him. His manner provided a perfect picture of knowledge and experience as well as a confirmed expectancy of victory.

Morphie's show of confidence added to Deloris' anxiety. His mouth now felt as dry as a soda cracker on a cold winter morning. Moreover, a secretion coated the back of his throat, producing a tickling sensation. He suppressed an urge to clear his throat for as long as he could but found himself unable to delay doing so any longer. With an eye fixed on Madam Meanness and a balled fist pressed against his mouth, he hawked twice before emitting a loud and guttural "auguuguugrrghh" as he undertook a throat-clearing maneuver.

Deloris' action earned him a squint and an intimidating scowl from the old woman. She pointed a long, slender finger at a stack of paper cups and a water pitcher on his counsel table and gestured for Deloris to drink some water.

Deloris smiled an apologetic thank-you to the clerk. He received only a prolonged glare in return.

Deloris lifted the pitcher and tilted it to pour water into a cup right at the moment two loud knocks on a door behind the bench fractured the semi-quiet of the room. The sound so startled Deloris his pour missed the cup entirely. The spilled water spread across the table onto the yellow pad upon which he had written his notes for oral argument.

As the court bailiff delivered the court cry and announced the opening of the June 1970 Term, Deloris jumped to his feet along with Billy Joe. Too scared to move, he watched his notes dissolve and blue-colored water inch toward him. He stole a look at the clerk of court and nodded at the spilled water as an appeal for help. The clerk only glared at him with gritted teeth and tilted head as water made it to the edge of the counsel table and dripped onto the carpet below.

"Now look what you did," Billy Joe said beneath his breath.

When the court cry concluded, the chief judge, a bald, bulldog of a man who sat in the middle of the three-member court, rolled back his chair and invited all present to be seated.

With Madam Meanness glowering at Deloris with an even more menacing expression than before, he, full of panic, tore off several pages from the back of his yellow pad and handed a couple of sheets to Billy Joe. Deloris dropped below the table to sop up the water on the carpet while Billy Joe attended to the table top. If the judges noticed what had happened, they did not disclose it.

"All right, Madam Clerk, if you will call the first case," the chief judge said.

The clerk stood. "The first case, Your Honors, is entitled *Ginger Childree versus James Holcomb*. It is an appeal from the

Court of Common Pleas. The appellant Ginger Childree is represented by Deloris Meek and the respondent by Etheridge Morphie, III, . . . Esquire."

"All right, Mr. Meek, we'll be happy to hear from you," the chief judge said.

There came a pause.

The chief judge stood halfway and leaned over the bench, looking about. "Mr. Meek?"

Deloris, on his knees below his counsel table, peeped at the chief judge, his eyes barely above the table top. "Yes, sir."

"What are you doing on the floor, sir?" the chief judge asked, his face one of bewilderment. He glanced around at the other two judges and back at Deloris. "Are you sick or something?"

"No . . . no, sir," Deloris managed to say as he scrambled to his feet.

"In that case, sir, what are you doing on the floor?"

"I'd . . . I'd . . . uh . . . spilt a little water, and I was trying to get . . . trying to, doncha you know, trying to . . . uh get it up, Your Honor."

As Billy Joe sneaked back into his chair, Deloris slipped from around the table, his heart pounding so hard against his chest he thought it might pop the buttons on his shirt. He stepped toward the lectern, gulping large quantities of air while carrying a yellow pad that dripped blue water onto the carpet as he came forward. As he neared the lectern, he noticed the associate judge to the left of the chief judge shaking his head while the one on the chief judge's right side, devoid of any expression, rested his head on hands folded as if in prayer. The chief judge simply sat staring at him, his head cocked and his mouth agape as he waited for Deloris to launch into his argument.

Deloris angled his head toward his own counsel table. "I'm sorry, Your Honors. I didn't mean to do it," he said, his voice trembling, his hands in motion. "I . . . uh—"

"We'll attend to it later," the chief judge said. "Don't worry about that right now. Tell us what brings you here, sir."

Troubles and Kuddles

"Yes, sir," Deloris said, swallowing. He glanced at the dark blue trail on the carpet. It led back to his counsel table. The sight nauseated him.

Somehow, he managed to speak. "Well, sir," he said, his hands making loops, "I brought this claim and delivery action against this preacher fella about a year or so ago. I represent the lady sitting there on the first row, Miss Ginger Childree—the pretty little lady in the pink suit—the one with the long, auburn hair. She used to do a ventriloquist act, her and this other person, but they broke up after she went into the ministry. Her and Kuddles, they did, I mean. Kuddles—she or it—I'm not ever sure about how you refer to it—anyway them two, they joined up with this tent preacher, Brother Jimmy Holcomb—he's the one she sued. Well, anyway, Ginger, she traveled all over with him, helping out with his revivals and such and doing a children's ministry. He's represented, Brother Holcomb is, by Mr. Morphie, the elderly gentleman sitting behind me at the other table, Your Honors."

Deloris' chest swelled large as he inhaled.

"Well, like I was saying, Ginger was a part of Brother Holcomb's ministry and about a year and a half ago, Brother Holcomb, after they got done with a revival there in North Carolina, the next morning real early he took off, leaving Miss Childree behind in her trailer. To add insult to injury, he ran off with her dummy. Later on, she come to me, asking for some help. We finally located him. Lucky for my client, he was holding a revival here in our state, Brother Holcomb was. Soon as I learned about where he was at, I brought this claim and delivery action to get the dummy back for Ginger—Miss Childree.

"To make a long story short, when we got around to trying it, it was a swearing contest. It was Brother Holcomb's word against Miss Childree's. Anyway, we lost. The trial judge, he said he'd believe a man of God over an actress any day. That's why come he found for Brother Holcomb. I tried to tell him Ginger wasn't no actress. I told him her and her dummy, they were child evangelists, and he said, 'Well, she used to be an actress,' and he didn't care what she was now. He said, 'once an actress, always an actress,' and something about original sin, which I didn't quite get, to be honest with Your Honors."

As Deloris started to say something else, the associate judge on the chief judge's right, an old, gray man, raised a trembling, thin hand with tentacle-like fingers, to signal Deloris not to speak. The associate judge spoke so softly Deloris held a hand to his ear, straining to hear him. "Mr. Meek," he warbled in a weak voice, "are you familiar with the standard of review we are to apply here?"

"The what, sir? The standard—"

The associate judge's voice grew a little louder. "The standard of review—the rule we, as appellate judges, must use in determining the outcome of an appeal in a law case. One like this one."

Deloris turned around and looked at Billy Joe who only raised his hands and arched his shoulders.

"I'm not sure," Deloris said, facing the court once again.

The associate judge sighed while the other members of the panel smiled. "I didn't think you did. I read your brief, and it is nothing more than a factual argument rehashing, it appears to me, the same one you made to the trial judge, who didn't buy a word of it. He chose to believe Reverend Holcomb and not believe Miss Childree, which was his prerogative for whatever reason."

"No, sir, he didn't believe her. He sure didn't. And that's why come we're appealing to you all. You know, like I heard a fella say one time, 'fair's fair and right's right and wrong's wrong.'"

"And rules are rules," the chief judge added.

The associate judge closed his eyes. "Mr. Meek, the standard of review we must apply in this case since it is a law case and not one in equity," he said, opening his eyes, "is the 'any evidence' standard. This means, if there is any lawful evidence that reasonably supports the factual findings of the trial judge, we must affirm those findings. As I read the record, sufficient lawful evidence reasonably supports the judge's findings that your client made an *inter vivos* gift of the dummy to the reverend, which is to say, she gave him the dummy. Such being the case, he therefore committed no wrong in taking it with him when he left. Simply put, it was a gift among the living—"

"But that's just it, Your Honor. She didn't give it to—"

"Sir, he testified she did. She said she didn't. The judge believed him. He didn't believe her. That, Sir, is evidence. You should know that. The reverend's testimony is evidence, Sir, and it supports the trial judge's finding of lawful possession. End of story."

"It is? But it's not fair, Your Honor. She testified he stole it from her."

Deloris turned and offered Billy Joe a helpless look.

The chief judge picked up the two briefs and laid them atop the record. He smiled at Deloris as he fastened a rubber band around the three documents. "Anything else, counsel?"

The associate judge on the chief judge's left spoke before Deloris could answer. "Before you sit down, Counsel, who is this Kuddles person? Is she the person sitting next to Miss Childree?"

Deloris looked around at the front row followed by a look back at the judges. "Oh, no sir, Your Grace. She's Mr. Pratt's secretary, Dixie St. John. Kuddles, she's what we're fighting Brother Holcomb over."

The chief judge turned to the associate judge, a much younger man than he and the other associate judge, and whispered in his ear. The associate judge laughed.

"Oh yes. Yes, of course," the associate judge responded, still laughing. "I'd forgotten. These cases, they all kinda run together. I'm sorry . . ."

"Yes, sir," Deloris said. "But yeah, we're fighting over Kuddles—you know, the dummy."

"Who are you calling a dummy, sir?" said the older associate judge, his head tilted toward Deloris and his brow furrowed. "I don't think name-calling is appropriate here."

"I'm not calling nobody a 'dummy,' " Deloris answered. "Well, Kuddles. She—I mean it—she's a real dummy, a kind of a doll, doncha know."

The chief judge, chuckling, leaned toward the old man as if preparing to say something to him. But the latter raised an open hand, apparently terminating any effort by the chief judge to speak to him.

"A kind of a doll? Pretty, you mean?"

The chief judge rolled his eyes while the younger associate judge held a hand to his mouth.

Ignoring the two other judges, Deloris attempted to answer the question asked him by the older one. "Well, yes, sir, Your Honor. You could call her pretty, I suppose. But to me, though, she's more kinda cute than what I'd call, you know, pretty or good looking. But that's just my opinion, if Your Honor please."

The elderly judge threw up his hands and looked toward the ceiling. "He waved his hand and shook his head. "Please continue, sir," he said with a sigh.

Before Deloris could proceed further with his argument, the three judges grouped together and held a brief conversation, while glancing Dixie's way every now and again and smiling. Deloris could not fault them for looking at Dixie, beautiful as she appeared and dressed, as she was, in a short-sleeve, short-length white dress with decorative buttons and matching parallel, broken lines. But more to the point, she sat with her long, shapely legs on stunning display.

"I'm sorry, Mr. Meek," the chief judge said. "Anything else, sir?"

"No, sir. I don't reckon."

"Very good. Mr. Morphie?"

Morphie leapt to his feet and paraded to the podium, his head held high, his hands empty of briefs and other papers. "Yes, Your Honor?"

"The three of us have agreed there's no need for us to hear from you."

The other two judges nodded in apparent agreement.

The chief judge smiled at Deloris. "It's pretty obvious, Mr. Meek, your appeal is completely without merit. We'll issue a Rule 220 order sometime this afternoon, confirming this."

Deloris hung his head. "Yes, sir," he muttered.

"Whether we agree or not with how the lower court ruled does not make any difference. We could not change the result if we disagreed with it, our standard of review being the way it is. We hope you understand, sir."

"Yes, sir," Deloris mumbled.

His head held low, Deloris dragged himself back to his counsel table as the chief judge beckoned the clerk of court to approach the bench.

The judges held another conference, this time with the clerk's participation. For the first time, Deloris saw Her Meanness smile, and she did so when she took a quick look his way. Her smile was so wide, Deloris would later swear, it stretched all the way around her head.

"One more thing, Mr. Meek," said the chief judge, the conference over.

"Yes, sir?"

"In addition to the court costs, including attorney fees, which we think you personally should bear and not pass on to your client, you will be billed for the costs involved in the cleaning up the mess you made on the carpet. You'll get a written order once we find out what the clean-up costs are."

As the judges stood to vacate the bench, Morphie, still standing, addressed them in a tone of voice that marked his snobbish demeanor. "Thank you, Your Honors. And if I may say so, it is always a pleasure to appear before such learned and wise men and do please give each of your wives my most affectionate personal regards. Sometime soon, my wife Carolyn and I would love to have the whole court for dinner and cocktails. If not here, perhaps at our beach house. Again, thank you."

Morphie threw a thumb over his shoulder aimed at Deloris. "I'm sorry you had to listen to such as this here. I know you have more important work to do."

"That's what we're paid to do, Mr. Morphie," the chief judge said. He glanced one last time at Dixie and grinned. "But I assure you, sir, of one thing. All has not been lost this morning. Even in the worst of cases, one might find some measure of pleasure."

***

Deloris sat with his large frame parked beside Billy Joe on the outside of a booth at the Bottom Feeder, an all-you-can-eat fish camp on the bank of a small lake near the capital city. Ginger sat opposite Deloris and Dixie sat across from Billy Joe. While Billy Joe and Dixie dove into their large servings of fried baby catfish, French fries, slaw, raw onions, and hush puppies, Deloris picked at his food, taking only an occasional sip of his sweet ice tea. For her part, Ginger nibbled on a hush puppy.

"You gonna eat that, Deloris?" Billy Joe said, pointing at Deloris' stacked platter.

"I swear, Billy Joe, I don't know where you put it all," Deloris responded. "The last time we ate here, you didn't eat a platter of catfish. No, you ate a whole durn school of them. I'm surprised they'll still let you in the place. I don't see how you stay so thin? I've never seen anybody who can put away food like you can do."

"Well, you gonna eat it or not?"

Deloris shoved the platter toward Billy Joe. "Here, help yourself. I don't feel like eating it no way. I'm still too upset. I shouldn't've ordered me anything. I believe I'll just have them bring me a Black Label, provided we can get the waitress to ever look our way."

"Ginger," Deloris said, "I've been mulling over your situation while we've been sitting here."

"Uh-oh," Billy Joe said. "You better watch out, Ginger."

Deloris ignored his remark. "I want you to think about something, okay? All that's happened to you here is this. You have—we have, and I mean 'we'—lost a court case and you've lost a dummy. That's all you've lost. Nothing else. You've still got your talent. You still can do ventriloquism. You can still do your work for the Lord. This dummy you lost, how much did she—it cost you? Guess what. You can still get you another one made. You can—"

"But, Deloris," Ginger said, her voice breaking, "a new one won't be Kuddles. Kuddles, she was like a daughter to me. She was special. I called her 'my first-made.' You know, like a mother's 'first-born.' Yes, she could be smart-mouth, even foul-mouth at times, but she could also be as sweet as—"

"I can't believe what I'm listening to," Dixie said, butting in. "Do either of you two wrecker-riders—"

Billy Joe interrupted. "I'm the one who rides the wreckers. Deloris, he chases the ambulances. He's got a truck, you know."

Dixie stomped on Billy Joe's foot.

"Oh!" he exclaimed. Billy rubbed his foot against the calf of his leg. "That hurt, Dixie."

"I meant it to. You shouldn't interrupt me," she said. "Like I was fixing to say, do either of you two hear what this woman's saying? Do you? She talks about that thing like it had flesh and blood."

Dixie turned to her seatmate. "Can't you get it through your head, Ginger, your dummy wasn't anything but a big ol' doll? A big ol' doll, for goodness sake." She paused and slammed back against the booth. "Geez. Pass me the ketchup, Billy Joe."

Ginger whimpered. "That's what she may be to you, Dixie, but to me she was real. Real, I tell you. Real as anybody. She was my buddy, my friend—my best friend. Somebody to talk to whenever I was in the dumps or worried about something."

"Believe me, honey, you're in serious need of some help," Dixie said, twirling her finger at her temple.

"Don't pay any attention to her, Ginger. She doesn't appreciate about how attached you ventriloquists can get to y'all's little people," Deloris said.

"Little people," Dixie harrumphed. "They're dolls, Deloris. Dolls—not little people."

Deloris ignored Dixie and offered Ginger a sad smile. "I'm not kidding, Ginger, contact the folks who made Kuddles and get them to make you another one."

"I tell you, Deloris, you don't know what you're missing," Billy Joe said, his mouth full. They've outdone themselves this time. These catfish—man, they're outta this world delicious. They're 'e-malicious.' Why, they'd make you wanna fight your grandma." He turned to Dixie. "You through with the ketchup?"

She slid the bottle across to him. "Pass it back when you're done. I like lotsa ketchup on everything."

Billy Joe wiped his mouth. "Yeah. I know. Even tomatoes."

Ginger patted the side of her eyes with her fingertips. "I'm sorry. I know y'all don't understand about Kuddles and me. I can't explain it myself. I loved her more than anything. I loved doing her voice, being her. I mean, people love their dogs and cats, they talk to them, cry when they get run over or get sick or something—treat them like family. That's the way it was with Kuddles and me. I looked on her as family. Sometimes, I think she was my other 'me'—my *alter ego*, as it were."

Billy Joe laid a set of skeletal catfish remains onto a growing pile of similar bones in the middle of the table. He reached for another catfish. "You know, listening to you, Ginger, it reminded me of something. I once had this client. I got her a divorce from this fella. He was a sorry thing, her husband was—"

"Aren't they all?" Dixie interrupted to say.

Billy Joe closed his eyes and sighed. "As I was about to say before I was so rudely interrupted, the husband was all the time beating up on my client, running around on her, drinking, not working half the time. Well, she would sit and cry whenever she'd come to my office and tell me all about what he'd been doing to her. After telling me about how low down he was—and using just about a whole box of tissues while she was doing it—she'd tell me how much she loved him and everything."

"What's your point?" Deloris said.

Billy Joe bit a hunk out of his catfish, chewed it a moment or two, and swallowed it. "My point? It's this." He took a sip of his tea. "I got her a divorce, and you know what? Why, within six months' time she was married again and happy as a tick on a hound dog, as the saying goes."

"So, you're agreeing with me, I take it," Deloris said.

"For once in my life, yeah I am," Billy Joe said. He nodded toward Deloris. "Like he said, get you another dummy, Ginger."

A quiet settled around the booth for a moment, lifted only when Ginger sniffed a couple of times and inquired of Deloris whether he knew of Holcomb's whereabouts at the present time.

Deloris shook his head. "I thought he'd be at the hearing this morning, but I didn't see him. But to tell the truth, I was so nervous and scared, the President of the United States of America, he could've been sitting out there in the courtroom and I wouldn't have seen him."

"I was kinda hoping he'd show and bring Kuddles with him," Ginger said. "I so much wanted to see her, and maybe talk to him again about her."

"I guess the reason Holcomb didn't come is Morphie doesn't believe in bringing a client to an appellate court when he argues his case," Billy Joe said. "That's what he told me one time."

Deloris let pass Billy Joe's observation about Morphie. "The last I heard, Ginger, the reverend was still in the upstate, but he could've moved on from there by now, obviously. Tell you what, when we get back home, I call Mr. Morphie, and I'll ask him where he is and let you know what he says. Okay?"

Ginger did not answer. She sat with her shoulders pushed back and her jaw set.

Deloris squinted at Ginger. Something about her manner troubled him. "What? You're not planning on confronting him again about stealing Kuddles, are you?"

Ginger pushed her plate aside. It still held almost all of her food. "I thought I'd make one last try in a real nice way to try and get her back. And if he won't either give her back or sell her to me, I'll give some thought about doing what you've suggested I do. What's wrong with that?"

"Nothing, I don't reckon," Deloris said. "But it'll be a waste of time. He'll never give her back to you. You need to accept the ways things are. Get on with your life. That's what I think."

"And suppose you did get you a new dummy," Dixie said, "would you go back to doing church work or have you thought about maybe trying to find your old partner what's-his-name and resurrecting y'all's act?"

"His name is Wally Teal, but his real name is Eli—Eli Fromberg," Ginger said. "Oh, I couldn't go back to doing night clubs and things." Ginger looked away for a couple of seconds, her chin resting in her palm.

Ginger smiled as she looked around at Dixie. "You know, on second thought, maybe I could under the right circumstances. I have to say, though, I enjoyed the children's ministry work Kuddles and I had been doing. I absolutely did. It's one of the things I hate worse about what Brother Holcomb did to me. He deprived me of an opportunity to do something good, to bring Christ to little boys and girls. When he stole Kuddles from me, he robbed me of more than what you, Dixie, call a 'big ol' doll.' "

"But the way I understood it, Kuddles may still be doing it," Dixie said.

"If so, somebody else is talking for her," Ginger said. "And it's not me, and that's the difference."

CHAPTER TWO

Shortly before eight o'clock in the morning, Deloris pulled his mobile law office, a purple-painted, converted milk truck, into a parking space next door to Kingry Insurance. The makeover involved, among other things, his fitting the back part of the truck with a desk, an office chair, a bookshelf, a file cabinet, and two guest chairs. As for parking, Deloris had negotiated an arrangement with Kingry Insurance whereby it allowed him to rent three spaces in its adjoining parking lot. The agency also permitted him access to one of its telephone lines and a secretary whenever he required either, provided he pledged not to sue any of its clients during the pendency of the arrangement.

Deloris rolled down both the driver-side and passenger-side windows to take advantage of the cool air left by a moderate rain from the night before. The scent of raindrops still lingered outside.

Deloris hauled himself from the cab into the office portion of his truck and sat down at his desk to catch up on the mail he had collected earlier from his post office box.

One envelope he dreaded to open bore the return address of the court of appeals, the forum in which he had argued the month before, an experience he wanted to forget. Setting aside correspondence he figured only requested gifts of money, he opened the envelope from the capital city. The letter inside and an attached document did not request him to give money; instead, it ordered him to send it or face court sanctions. In addition to dismissing Ginger's appeal, the court directed a check for $615 be sent to its clerk in payment of court costs. The amount included attorney fees incurred by Brother Holcomb in responding to Ginger's appeal and the expense incurred by the court for carpet cleaning.

As Deloris pulled open the drawer in which he kept his check book, he heard a knock on one of the two back doors of his truck. His truck bounced. Deloris looked to his right and spotted the face of Oleander "Smudge" Chiselbrook framed by one of the rear-door windows as he peered inside, a hand to his beady eyes. Deloris saw the face disappear and, almost simultaneously with its disappearance, felt the truck bounce once more. Deloris reasoned

Smudge had jumped on the back bumper to look inside the truck and had hopped back onto the ground.

"Deloris? It's me, Smudge. Got a sec?" came a voice from outside his back doors.

Ordinarily, and like most of the other members of the local Bar, Deloris wanted nothing to do with Chiselbrook, a lawyer who always, it seemed, managed to escape disbarment no matter the allegations and evidence against him. Most Bar members regarded Chiselbrook not only as a fool, a clown, and a hopeless incompetent, but as a lawyer so crooked he could be used as an auger for well digging. Toleration of Chiselbrook's antics in the courtroom and his attitude regarding professional ethics evolved, in the main, from the type of clientele he ordinarily represented. They consisted of drunks, the mentally challenged, the mentally disturbed, the unemployable, the ex-cons, the tramps, and the other problematic outcasts of society. In short, his clients included those who queued up with other scorned souls on Monday mornings to be judged and jailed by the municipal court for minor offenses. These unfortunates would live all but forgotten were it not for their arrest records. Apparently, the powers-that-be had long ago decided somebody had to represent them, and who better than Smudge Chiselbrook. They deserved no better, so went the general feeling.

Deloris cursed to himself as he opened the door. "Yeah, Smudge," he said, "what is it? I'm kinda busy right now. If it's money you want, I don't have any. I gotta come up with a little over six hundred dollars my ownself, doncha know."

Smudge, a short, feisty fellow, ran a hand through his stock of red hair. "I ain't here to hit you for no money, Deloris." He patted his front pocket. "Pickings been real good for me this morning at city court. I bet I made myself two hundred dollars. Hell, one guy I represented, know what? He had a hundred smackers hid out in his boot." Smudge laughed. "Tell you what. It ain't there no more. I got me most of it. The court, it got the rest. It's days like today which makes a fella love capitalism. You know, Deloris, we're the last of them."

"The last of who?"

Troubles and Kuddles

"The last of the capitalists, that's who."

"Well, if it's not money you want, what you want then?"

Smudge stepped backwards and over to the side of the truck. He waved his arm in a beaconing fashion, "You can come on around. Your buddy's right here." He turned toward Deloris. "Hey Deloris. Know this fella?"

A moment later a man, younger looking than those Smudge usually represented, walked around the corner of the truck into Deloris' presence. He carried a suitcase and one other travel case. The man, slim of build and with dark, curly hair and a beard, stopped beside Smudge and nodded at Deloris. "Good morning, Mr. Meek. Remember me, sir?"

Deloris stepped from his truck into the parking lot and approached Smudge's companion. His face tightened as he studied the bearded man for a few moments. Deloris eased back. "You look familiar, but I can't place you." He glanced at Smudge. "Care to tell me who this is, and why you brought him here?" Deloris crossed his arms as he kept his eyes on the stranger.

The man opened his mouth to speak, but Smudge spoke before he could do so. "Let me tell him, how 'bout it."

Smudge drew closer to Deloris, jerking his thumb over his shoulder. "My buddy here, he's the one who had the hundred on him." He laughed. "While me and him was waiting for them to call his case, I got to talking with him some, asking him what he was doing around here and so forth. Know what he told me? He said he was looking for him a lawyer who went by a girl's name. I told him we didn't have no girl lawyers in town. He said the lawyer he was looking for was a man, not no woman. I said I didn't know no lawyer like that neither, but we did have two or three sissyfied lawyers." He laughed again and pinched Deloris on his arm. "You know who I'm talking about, doncha?"

Deloris rubbed his arm. "Not really."

"Oh you do," Smudge said. "Anyway, all of a sudden like, your name, it kinda popped in my head. I said, 'Come to think of it, I might know what lawyer you're talking about. Is he a kinda pear-shaped fella and goes by the name of Deloris, only he spells his name with a 'i' and not with no 'e.'

"He said the name kinda sounded like him and asked me what his last name was, and I said it was 'Meek'—you know like in the Bible where it says the 'meek shall inherit the earth' kinda meek. When I said this, he asked me if the lawyer I knew practiced law out of a milk truck. I told him yeah, you could say that, only it wasn't no milk truck no more. After I said this, he said 'That's him, yep that's him, all right—Deloris Meek.' "

Deloris pushed Smudge to the side and looked again at the strange young man. "Wally? Is it really you, Wally? Wally Teal?"

The young man dropped his head. "Yes, sir. Remember, you gave me a ride once—well, actually it was two of us—Ginger Childree and me. Remember?"

***

Because of the spring-like fall weather, Deloris opted to chat with Wally outdoors. Deloris spread two lawn chairs in the shade of the insurance building next door. He placed them on the far side of his truck, away from the sidewalk and street to offer him and Wally more privacy and to mute somewhat the noise from the traffic, pedestrian and motor vehicle. Smudge left soon afterward, apparently taking a hint he should leave Deloris and Wally alone since Deloris brought out only two chairs and invited Wally to sit in one chair as he took the other for himself.

"What'd you do after you left the Polk Inn?" Deloris asked.

His reference was to the motel in which Wally, Ginger, and he had stayed in Louisiana after they first met. The Polk Inn sat across the highway from Brother Jimmy Holcomb's revival tent. The last Deloris had seen of Wally had been the evening when both he and Wally had been assaulted at the Bayou Pickin' Parlor during a performance by Wally and Ginger of a ventriloquist act with their puppets Kody and Kuddles.

A heckler had charged onto the stage after Wally directed an unflattering remark at the heckler in response to an insult. The heckler jerked Kody from Wally's hands and pounded him with it as he lay on the stage floor. Deloris attempted to rescue Wally but failed in the effort when Kody's head flew off during the attack and smacked Deloris full in the face. The blow had knocked him down the steps onto the dance floor where a couple whom he presumed to be a prostitute and her pimp attacked him, kicking him about the face and upper body. Deloris had earlier reproved the woman and slapped her hand away when she rubbed her hand on his leg in an obvious invitation for him to join her in an intimate, fee-based relationship.

"What did I do after I left Shreveport? I caught a bus and returned home to New Jersey. I got me a sales job with a plumbing company. I worked there until a few months ago when I decided I should try and find Ginger and maybe persuade her to leave what she was doing and agree to revive our act. Since leaving New Jersey, I've been doing odd jobs here and there, waiting tables, day labor, pretty much anything to get by while I looked for her."

"What happened here? How'd you wind up in jail?"

Wally hung his head. "They said vagrancy. I had merely sat down on a bench outside the courthouse to rest a minute or two last Saturday afternoon. This man in a navy-blue suit came walking by while I was sitting there. I stopped him to ask if he knew a lawyer who drove a milk truck. He looked at me like I was crazy, said something like 'You want to know whether I know a lawyer who runs a milk route?' He cursed at me and walked on off, mumbling to himself. After he walked about fifteen or twenty yards, I saw him stop a policeman and point at me. Next thing you know, the policeman had me in handcuffs and had me thrown in jail. I couldn't believe it. I tried talking to him, but he pointed his billy club at me, and told me to shut my mouth and not say another word.

"This morning when they brought all of us into the courtroom, Mr. Chiselbrook asked if anybody wanted a lawyer and said he was available. I raised my hand, and he asked me if I had any money. I'd never been arrested before. I didn't know what to do, so I told him I had a hundred dollars in my shoe. He said he reckoned that'd do, and he'd take what the court didn't. He said my sentence would probably be $30 or 30 days. And that's exactly what it was—$30 or 30 days. So, I paid the court $30, and Mr. Chiselbrook, he got what was left over, leaving me completely broke."

Deloris rubbed his chin and studied Wally for a moment. "I hate to tell you this, but the judge would've given you the same sentence anyway, lawyer or no lawyer."

Wally's eyes blinked. "Honest? If I had've known—"

"Well, all that's water under the bridge. Forget about it. How'd you end up here?"

Wally held his breath a moment. He made eye contact with Deloris. "I remembered you saying something about practicing law in this state, but for the life of me I couldn't remember the name of the town. I thought I'd look for you all over the state, inquiring about a lawyer who practiced law out of a milk truck and had a girl-sounding name. I decided I'd continue searching for you until I found you. I also kept on the lookout for anything which might indicate Holcomb's whereabouts. I figured where I found him, I'd find her too."

Deloris tilted back in his chair. "I can tell you a little something about Ginger. Until recently, I represented her, even had to go before the court of appeals up yonder at the capital."

"You did?" Wally said, his eyes wide and his voice exuding excitement.

Deloris' shoulders drooped. "We lost."

"Oh." Wally frowned, shaking his head. "I'm sorry."

"Well, me too." Deloris pressed his hands to his temples. "About all I can only tell you is her last phone number and mailing address. I got it inside my truck on my organizer. Whether they're still good or not, I hadn't got the foggiest idea, though she did promise to let me know of any changes. But it's been a while since I last laid eyes on her or heard from her. She said she was going go look for Holcomb and offer to buy Kuddles back from him if he wouldn't give her back."

"Buy Kuddles back? She sold Kuddles?"

"Naw. Holcomb took off and left her high and dry in North Carolina and stole Kuddles from her in the process. Well, according to her, he stole Kuddles. He claimed Ginger sold her to him, though personally, I can't see her doing that. Anyway, she came to me for legal help, and I brought suit against the good reverend for claim and delivery—"

"Claim and delivery?"

"Yeah. It's what we call a legal action to get back somebody's personal property which somebody else wrongfully took from them. In other words, I sued Holcomb to try and get Holcomb to return Kuddles to Ginger." Deloris sighed. "Like I said, we lost. I told her she probably ought to get her another dummy and forget all about Kuddles. I know that's what I'd do, if I were her." Deloris' chin dropped, and he shook his head. "But she wouldn't hear of it."

"I'm not surprised. She was extremely attached to Kuddles." Wally looked off into the distance a few seconds. "I didn't know she and Holcomb had terminated their relationship. First I've heard about that." Wally's eyes danced as he sat up straight. "Fact is, though, Mr. Meek, it's the most encouraging news I've had lately."

"Encouraging?"

"Yes, sir. The fact they're no longer together improves my chances of convincing her to resurrect our act, Kuddles or no Kuddles. Tell me, you have any idea about where Holcomb might be now?"

"You still figure you might find Ginger there too?"

"Yes, sir, since you indicated she planned to try again to recover Kuddles from that preacher somehow. What you told me is the only lead I have."

"Right now, I don't know for sure where Holcomb is. His lawyer told me the last time I spoke with him he was holding forth and saving souls in Awenasa. That's a small mill town upstate, not far from Greenfield, about a hour-and-a-half ride from here. I think he figures he found himself a home. He's been there for a good while. If Ginger did go to Awenasa like she said she was going to do, I guess she still may be there since, as I said, I haven't heard from her lately."

Wally stood and picked up his bags.

"Going someplace?" Deloris said, getting to his feet.

Wally swept his arms around. "Why, to look for Ginger, of course."

"You don't have to go right yet, do you?" He nudged Wally, smiling. "Tell you what, why don't you stay with me tonight? You can get yourself all cleaned up real good, and I'll take you out to dinner. How 'bout it?"

Wally closed his eyes a moment and waved both hands. "You don't have to do that, Mr. Meek. Haven't they got a Y.M.C.A. here in town? I could probably stay at it. I've stayed at some of them before. Tell you what. If you really want to do something for me, you could maybe loan me fifty dollars or so, which I'll pay you back as soon as I land a job somewhere."

The loan request distressed Deloris somewhat. He drew in a deep breath as he thought about the matter. He did not want to loan Wally the funds, but his conscience would not permit him to refuse to do so, especially since Smudge—a fellow lawyer— had taken the last penny the poor man had. Deloris knew already he would have to borrow money to pay the costs ordered by the court of appeals. Now, he would have to borrow even more if he gave in to Wally's request.

Wally continued. "One other thing you might could do for me is ride me out to the highway in the morning so I can hitchhike to—what's the name of the place again?"

"Awenasa, a little town near Greenfield." Deloris looked at his watch and reached for his wallet from which he withdrew two twenties and a ten. "Here, Wally. Take this. Pay me back when you can."

Wally's head dropped and his Adam's apple rose and fell as the money changed hands. "Thank, you Mr. Meek. You've never been anything but kind to me."

"I wanna do it, Wally. But you got me wrong. Truth to tell, I should not have left you in Shreveport like I done. I still feel bad about leaving you there all by yourself, and you all beat up. At the time, I didn't think I had me much of a choice. I had some important business I had to attend to, which was why I was going to Texas to start with. So, I'd kinda like to make amends for doing you like I did, if you'll let me. How about it? Will you spend the night at my place?"

Wally kicked at the ground. "I don't know. I hate to put—"

"Wally, you really don't have much of a choice, to be honest. We don't have a Y.M.C.A. So, it's either stay with me or find you a boxcar. Besides, if you'll spend the night with me, it'll give us a chance to talk some more, and I can fill you in on all what's happened since I last saw you." Deloris smiled, leaned toward Wally, and lowered his voice. "And I know you'd just love to hear about Dixie, now wouldn't you?"

"Dixie?" Wally laughed. "You mean the gorgeous woman we left at the bus stop that night shortly after you picked Ginger and me up when we were out hitchhiking?"

Deloris grimaced as he well remembered his abandoning Dixie. "Yeah. One and the same. Dixie St. John. She's just as beautiful and as difficult as ever, doncha know. We might've told y'all when we were all getting acquainted, she worked for another lawyer—Billy Joe Pratt. She wasn't working for me. She was merely along for the ride. I was supposed to have dropped her off at her hometown, but when we got there, she changed her mind and insisted on going with me to Texas."

"To Abilene, wasn't it?"

Deloris nodded. "Getting back to Pratt, Dixie's boss. He practices here in town. He's a good ol' boy. We've been friends since law school. He helps me sometime—well, sorta helps me."

Deloris checked the time again. "Tell you what. I'd love to talk to you some more right now, but in a few minutes I've got me an appointment with the loan department around the corner." He flashed his teeth. "Just wait here till I get back. If you wanna, you can sit out here or go sit in my truck. Choice is yours. Anyway, I'm gonna leave it with you, and if anyone should come looking for me, tell them I'll be back in about hour or so."

CHAPTER THREE

The next morning, Deloris headed for Kingry's Insurance office where he inquired about telephone messages. No one had called. *Par for the course*, he thought.

Before leaving to return to his truck, Deloris thanked the secretary who handled his telephone messages and promised to take her to lunch sometime soon. He frequently made her this promise but never kept it.

His "don't-sue promise" to Harvey Kingry, the agency's owner, sometimes proved costly. Billy Joe Pratt had once brought suit against a Kingry insured for an automobile accident victim whom Deloris had turned away because of the agreement. Pratt recovered a five-figure verdict for the man. Worst, Pratt never let Deloris forget it, often adding when he reminded Deloris of his good fortune, "You ought to get rid of that dumb truck and get yourself a real office. Whoever heard of anybody practicing law out of a milk truck in the first place? You'd done better to've used your truck for a milk route, if you ask me."

Deloris had responded, saying "I didn't ask you."

No sooner had Deloris closed the door behind him when leaving Kingry's Insurance than he heard a familiar voice call his name. He turned around and spotted Dixie St. John about thirty yards away. She wore a knitted, soft-yellow, skinny-rib, long-sleeve turtleneck sweater with a matching skirt. The hem of the skirt dropped to about an inch above her knees. Brown pumps complemented her outfit. A leather purse of a similar brown hung from her shoulder.

Deloris watched and waited as she advanced toward him, her hips swaying to and fro in rhythmic fashion as she took long strides. Being Dixie epitomized "head-turner" females throughout the whole earth, every man she passed on the sidewalk spun around to eyeball her further. Deloris surmised each of them entertained lustful thoughts about Dixie, judging from the way their eyes followed her, thus committing the sin of the heart, an action Jesus condemned in *Matthew* 5:28.

Deloris could not help but laugh when he remembered a conversation he and Billy Joe Pratt had about this particular sin. Pratt deemed it grossly unfair for the Lord to create something so pleasing to the eye as a beautiful woman and also make it a mortal sin to want her in a carnal way. He said God's creation of gorgeous females and His allowing them to parade about in the presence of the male species amounted to entrapment, a defense at common law but apparently unavailable for after-death judgment proceedings.

When Dixie got to Deloris, she punched him on the upper arm.

"Ouch!" he said, rubbing where she had struck him and looking around to gage the reactions of walk-bys. "What'd you hit me for anyway?"

"Because I saw you last night and waved to you, and you didn't wave back."

"But I didn't see you last night," he said, shaking his head. "Where'd you see me at?"

"You and some little bearded guy, y'all were coming out of Gregorio's. Mama and I, we were across the street on our way to the picture show, and we saw you."

"I'm sorry. I didn't mean to ignore y'all." He gave her a look. "I bet you don't know who the fella was who was with me, do you? You'd never guess it in a million years."

Dixie tilted her head to the side. "Who?"

"You remember the fella who was with Ginger the time we gave them a lift when they were out hitchhiking?"

"You mean you gave them a lift," Dixie said in a cutting tone. "If you will recall, I told you not to do it. But no, you went right on ahead and did it. And look what happened to you later on? You got your big fanny whipped to a fare-thee-well—and by a prostitute no less, in a durn juke joint, of all places."

Deloris laughed, but not hard. "My fanny? No, huh-uh." He rubbed his brow. "It was more like my noggin. And it wasn't only the prostitute, neither. She had her some help. Anyhow that's who was with me last night—the fella with Ginger, her partner in their ventriloquist act, Wally Teal. Only his real name isn't 'Wally.' It's 'Eli Fromberg.' He uses 'Wally Teal' as his stage name—least he used to. I still called him 'Wally.' Ginger Childree calls him that too."

"What's he doing here?"

"Looking for Ginger, he told me. He says he's had it pretty hard since me and him got beat up in Shreveport. He's been doing odd jobs here, there, and yonder while trying to find her. I let him stay with me last night and saw him off at the bus station this morning. Plus, I loaned him some money, poor guy." He nodded toward a café across the street. "Got time for some coffee?"

Dixie glanced at her watch. "No, I better get on to the office. Your buddy Lawyer Pratt gets a mite nervous if I'm even one minute late." She frowned. "Like he's got a whole lot to do. He spends more time at my desk than at his own. Not that I'm ever busy. But if he's willing to pay me to sit around and twirl the carriage on my Underwood, it's perfectly all right with me. It's his money."

"How was the movie y'all went to see, you and your mama?"

"Dreadful."

Deloris' lips puckered. "Oh, that's too bad." His eyes widened and his mouth opened slightly. "Tell you what, how about me and you catching a movie at the drive-in tonight?"

"What's playing?"

Deloris rolled his tongue against his cheek and laughed. "Now, if what's playing matters, I'm not sure I wanna take you."

Dixie's nose wrinkled. "If what's playing doesn't matter, I most certainly do not wanna go. Not with you, I don't." She shifted her purse from one shoulder to the other. "I gotta get on. See you later. I'll tell Billy Joe you said hello."

"You'd be lying."

"I know. Before I went to work for him, I used to not do it—you know, lie. But if you tell folks when they call and ask to speak to Billy Joe, like I have to do all day long, 'he's in conference,' after a while it gets pretty doggone easy for me to lie about everything else. I'm durn near an expert at lying by now. Heck, I ought to apply for me a law license."

Deloris watched her walk away, her rear end again into the swing of things. He suppressed a sinful thought of his own but perhaps too late for it not to be counted against him when it came his turn at the Great White Throne Judgment to answer for his transgressions.

At one time—on their way back from Texas after he and Dixie had formed a bond of sorts because of their work together in locating the heiress they had sought—he sensed he had a shot at her. Ginger's sudden appearance on the scene later on, however, had brought to a close any possibility of a romance developing between him and Dixie. He tried to explain to Dixie he harbored no romantic feelings for Ginger and the only thing she wanted from him was legal assistance; but Dixie refused to accord his explanation any credit at all.

Deloris heaved a sigh and sauntered to his mobile office, hopeful he could earn a few dollars during the next several hours. He managed to make it to the rear of his truck before someone hailed him. He wheeled around and saw a man with a cigar jammed in his mouth, walking, almost running toward him. The man wore a double-breasted, navy-blue suit and a dark-colored felt fedora hat with a red feather inserted in its band.

When the man arrived at the spot where Deloris stood, the man removed the cigar from his mouth and pointed it at Deloris. "Your name 'Meek'?" The man appeared out of breath and spoke with a Yankee accent.

Deloris studied the gentleman, wondering whether he was a process server or debt collector since the man had the look of either. Deloris decided to answer the man, hoping for the best. Yeah, I'm Deloris Meek. Can I help you, sir?"

With his free hand, the man removed a small leather case from a pocket inside his coat and flashed what appeared to Deloris to be credentials of some sort. He performed the maneuver so quickly Deloris had no time to read the card inside the ID holder.

The man extended his hand in greeting. "Name's Jaden Ziglar, but you can call me Jade. I'm a private detective, licensed in New Jersey. I was hoping to have a word with you."

Deloris took Ziglar's hand and shook it. "Private detective? New Jersey?"

"Right," the man growled.

Deloris took stock of the man. He guessed him to be in his early forties or late thirties. He placed his height at about five feet, four inches and his weight at around two hundred pounds. Had he not told him he was a private detective, Deloris would have supposed this stump of a fellow to be a gangster, judging from his Yankee accent and his clothes, particularly his fedora, black and white shoes, and the red silk handkerchief in the upper-left coat pocket of his suit.

"Can we talk, Mr. Meek?"

"Well, yeah. You wanna do it out here, or if you wanna, we can go inside my truck there. It's got an office in it. Whichever."

"The man shook his cigar at the truck and sneered. "You call that a law office?"

"Yes, sir." Deloris paused. "Wanna see inside?"

The man scratched beneath his chin with the hand holding the cigar. "Nah. Out here'll do fine. This won't take but a minute or two. And if you can help me, I'm authorized to pay you for the information."

The man now had Deloris' full attention. "Whatcha wanna know?" Deloris said, grinning.

Ziglar withdrew a photograph from an inside coat pocket. "I believe you might know the person on the left, do you not? I'm informed you've represented her recently."

He handed the picture to Deloris.

Deloris drew back the second he looked at it. He recognized it as a publicity photograph Ginger and Wally had used to promote their act. "Yeah," Deloris said after a bit more study, "I know both her and the man with her. I know the names of the dummies they've got sitting on their laps too. The woman is Ginger Childree, and she called her dummy Kuddles. The man on the right there, his name is Eli Fromberg, but he generally goes by his stage name, Wally Teal." His dummy was named Kody."

Deloris returned the photograph.

After Ziglar glanced at the picture, he squinted at Deloris. "Wanna know something, counselor?" he said, rubbing his mouth. "The boy dummy, it kinda favors you a little bit."

Deloris ignored the observation. "Whatcha wanna know if I know Ginger for? She do something wrong?"

Ziglar slipped the photograph back inside his coat without answering Deloris' question. "Have you seen Fromberg lately or have any idea where we might find him?"

"I thought you were interested in the woman. You know, Ginger."

"Fromberg left New Jersey sometime back. My client and I believe he's probably gone looking for the Childree woman. We understand she's been down here and, as I indicated, information reached us you had represented her in some kind of a lawsuit. We know she'd once been traveling with an evangelist. If we can find her, we'll more than likely find Fromberg. At least, we feel like we will."

Ziglar looked at Deloris out of the corner of his eye. "What can you tell us about them? Anything?"

Deloris balled his left hand and pressed his fist against his lips, trying to decide whether to tell the man what he knew or not. He decided to go for the money, having persuaded himself he owed no obligation to protect either Ginger's or Wally's identity or whereabouts.

"You just missed Wally or Fromberg or whatever you wanna call him, Mr. Ziglar. He spent last night with me, as a matter of fact."

Ziglar's face appeared to tighten. "Damn! He always seems to be one step ahead of me."

"He's not going far, sir. After breakfast early this morning, I took him by the Trailways station where he took a bus to Awenasa. That's a little town upstate, close to Greenfield. Last I heard Reverend Holcomb—he's the evangelist Ginger'd been travelling with—that's where he'd last set up his tent at and that's where I understood Ginger—Miss Childree—was going last I heard from her. She was gonna try and get back the dummy she claims Holcomb stole from her—you know, Kuddles, the girl dummy there in the picture you got."

Ziglar removed a pen and small tablet from another inside coat pocket, wrote something down, and put them back in his pocket. "Well, Mr. Meek, you've been a lot of help to me." Ziglar dug into his pants pocket and withdrew a roll of cash from which he peeled off four fifty-dollar bills. "Here's two hundred dollars, Mr. Meek—for your time this morning. I hope the amount is satisfactory."

Deloris did not know what to say. He nodded and mumbled a "yeah-sure." His hand trembled when he reached for the money.

Ziglar offered his right hand, which Deloris, without thinking, grabbed with his left one. Ziglar thanked him for the information and hurried off toward a late-model, black Cadillac with white-wall tires parked across the street from the Kingry Insurance parking lot.

As Deloris slipped the money into a pants pocket, he had some slight misgivings about his telling the detective what he did, particularly because Ziglar never told him why he sought Wally's whereabouts; but whether he did the right thing or not, the two hundred dollars warmed Deloris' thigh and he resolved not to worry about what he had done.

***

Deloris sat at his desk inside his truck to sort through the morning mail he'd earlier picked up from the post office. In addition to a *Life Magazine*, his mail included a request for money from the Salvation Army, an overdue utilities bill accompanied by a letter warning of a cutoff of the gas and electricity at his rental house if he failed to pay the bill within three days, and a letter from a disgruntled ex-client threatening to turn him in to the attorney grievance board for not returning telephone calls and answering correspondence. Deloris threw the letter into the waste can. With the two hundred dollars burning a hole in his pocket, he decided he best pay his electric and gas company bill while he still had funds to do it.

Afterward, Deloris spent the rest of the morning drafting a summons and complaint in a fender-bender case and going over a chiropractor's report detailing the injuries allegedly suffered by his client, Augustine Willis.

Deloris represented Willis on a contingency-fee basis. Willis' case presented some serious problems. He had been cited by the police for running a stop sign and causing the accident in question. His breath smelled of alcohol, prompting his arrest for driving under the influence. For his part, Willis denied running the stop sign and, even if he had done so, claimed the other fellow had sufficient time within which to avoid the collision. As for the alcohol odor, he swore to Deloris it was nothing more than mouthwash. He denied the allegation of drunkenness, telling Deloris, "I'm a Baptist and everybody knows we don't drink."

By bringing suit before the other motorist could sue Willis, Deloris hoped the latter's insurance carrier would retain him to defend a counterclaim Deloris fully expected the other motorist would plead as one of several defenses. Otherwise, Deloris recognized his work on the case most likely would go unrewarded. He knew the chance of Willis either recovering a verdict or obtaining a settlement stood somewhere between zero and one-hundred degrees below zero.

But he thought, *What the hell? At least I'll gain me some experience.*

As for "experience," an old lawyer had once told Deloris there was no substitute for it. After he opened his law practice, however, Deloris quickly found out there was indeed a important substitute for experience—money.

Deloris' empty stomach gnawed at him. He looked at his watch. Both hands pointed to the number twelve. He hankered for a Grease Pit hotdog, smothered in onions, chili, and served with a pint of ice-cold chocolate milk. He got into his truck and motored to the sandwich shop, a popular eatery catering primarily to the students who attended Cooper Junior College across the highway.

When he entered the cement-block building, the smell of raw onions, frying hamburger meat, and French-fried potatoes greeted his nostrils. He spotted an empty stool to the right of the cash register and mounted his large frame aboard its small round seat. To Deloris' right sat a college student, his nose buried in a physics text book.

"Studying physics, huh? You know the only thing I learned when I took physics in college?" Deloris said, trying to be witty.

"No, sir," said the student.

"What goes up must come down. So, let me ask you this. How come it don't work the other way around? You know, what goes down must come up."

"Some things do, as a matter of fact. Elevators. Submarines, to name two."

"Hmmm," Deloris hummed. "You're right. Boy, are you smart. You must be in graduate school."

"No, sir. Sophmore year."

"When I took physics in college, I didn't take the really hard kind like the engineering students had to do. We called the kind we history majors took 'Betty Crocker Physics.' I still found it hard."

"Who's Betty Crocker?"

Deloris smiled at the student. "I'm not sure. I believe she's the one wrote our physics book."

The young man smiled and returned to his study as Glory Hiers, a flabby, hard-face woman with short, gray hair and unpainted lips, stomped to the counter from the grill area at the open area of the U-shaped counter.

Curse words flowed from Glory's mouth like water from a turned-on spigot. They concerned something or someone Deloris could not make out. He presumed they likely had something to do with her husband. Glory's expletives and the fulminations she directed toward her husband served as one of the Grease Pit's principal attractions, another being its funny books, which like Glory's profanities and denunciations, were always in plentiful supply.

Glory owned the business with her husband Rufus. She ran the cash register at the bend of the counter and took orders. Rufus did everything else, plus endured never-ending complaints, criticisms, and curses from Glory. In her eyes, the poor man seemed unable to do anything right. How he managed to always look cheerful mystified Deloris. He and Billy Joe often debated how—not when—Rufus would murder Glory. They agreed he would do it while she slept, being he'd be too afraid of his wife to attempt killing her during her waking hours.

Troubles and Kuddles

"Why hello, Deloris, honey," Glory said, her voice honeysuckle sweet. "The son-bitch back there will be the death of me yet. The only thing he ever done right was to marry me. He took advantage of my situation when I was kinda vulnerable, you know right after I lost my fourth husband to the TB—although, to tell you the truth, I couldn't wait for him to die. I may not've told you, but it was his life insurance money what paid for this damn sorry place." She swept her arms all around.

Deloris had heard the story many times, in fact. So had the physics student, apparently, for his eyes never left his text book.

"Yeah, Glory. You've told me all that," Deloris said.

"Did I, honey? Oh, I'm sorry. I forgot I did. I blame Rufus—the sorry, no-count excuse for a man. He keeps me so upset, I can't remember nothing no more, sometimes not even my own name." She wiped her face with her white apron. "Tell you something I do remember. A fella, he come by here early this morning asking how he'd go 'bout finding you. Hope you don't mind me telling him how."

Deloris spun his seat more in her direction. "Was it a man in a blue suit, double-breasted?"

Before Glory could answer, Rufus yelled out a greeting from his post at the grill. Like Glory, he wore a white apron, but his was smeared with grease splatters. He also had on a cook's hat and stood with a spatula in his hand. "You just come in, Deloris?" he said, his smile adding to his already happy face, a face that often reminded Deloris of a circus clown.

"How many times I gotta tell you, you dumb ass," Glory roared, "I do the greeting in this joint, and you do the frying. Now you turn your butt around and go do whatcha supposed to do, else I'll fry your sorry ass. I swear to goodness. One of these days . . . "

Deloris had a thought. *The spatula. One day Rufus'll kill her with the spatula. He'll stick it right down her mouth or up her. . .* He didn't finish the thought.

Glory faced Deloris once more. "A man in a double-breasted blue suit? Yeah, as a matter of fact. He come in for a cup of coffee. I asked him why come he wanted to see you. Know what? He wouldn't say. He drunk his coffee durn near all of it at once—and it steaming hot. When he got done, he tossed a dollar bill down on the counter, told me to keep the change, and hauled his butt right on out."

"He's looking for a fella, that was all he wanted," Deloris said. "Somebody you wouldn't know. I hardly know him my ownself."

"Oh? Well, I wasn't trying to pry into his business. Just making conversation. I have to say, though, I didn't like his looks. And there was something about his attitude—coulda been 'cause he was a Yankee."

Glory placed her elbows on the counter and rested her chin in her hands. She gazed up at Deloris.

"Hey, Glory," Rufus called out, "tell him 'bout Dixie coming in here last night."

Glory stood and gave Rufus a look. "Shut up, willya? Hot damn! You the talkingest son-bitch I believe I ever saw. You could'n't keep your damn mouth shut, even if your life depended on it, can you?"

"What's this about, Dixie?" Deloris asked in an attempt to take the heat off Rufus.

She frowned at Deloris and batted the air. "Oh nothing. She come in here last night late. Her and Billy Joe did. Both of them got take out. Pie, I believe it was. Fact is, she bought two pieces. I told her she was gonna chunk up, if she wasn't careful." Glory stepped back and slapped both hips. "Like this here. Dixie, she kinda laughed and said she planned to watch what she ate but only until she got married, which wasn't gonna be no time soon. Later on, she said she was gonna eat whoever she married out of house and home and he'd have to do all the cooking, which would make him an accomplice."

The news of Dixie's and Billy Joe's late evening visit to the Grease Pit surprised Deloris. "Dixie came in here with Billy Joe? Last night, you say?"

"Yeah. They must've gone to the picture show. She told me not to go see the one playing right now at the Palace. Said it wasn't no good. Billy Joe, he said he didn't like it neither. I asked them when in the world would I have time to go to no picture show even if I wanted to. All I do is work here all the time, except when I go home to go to bed. If I ain't working, I'm sleeping. My bastard husband back there, why, he can work and sleep at the same time. Never seen nobody like him in all my born days, the son-bitch."

Deloris lost his appetite. What Glory related to him about Billy Joe and Dixie delivered any desire he had for food a death blow. If what she told him was the truth, he concluded, it meant Dixie had lied to him and he could not understand why she would do it.

"What can we get for you?" Glory asked. "You ain't said. How 'bout a Lubricator?"

The "Lubricator" represented the Grease Pit's signature meal, a generous serving of greasy French-fried potatoes and fried onion rings, and a thick, juicy hamburger steak cooked to order. A huge glass of a syrupy ice tea with which to wash it all down came with the meal.

Deloris eased off the stool. "No thank you, Glory. I almost forgot. I've got an appointment in a few minutes. I'll have to catch y'all later."

Deloris returned to his truck and drove back to his usual parking space next door to Kingry's Insurance. There he sat sulking behind his desk with his feet propped up and his arms behind his neck. He kept asking himself over and over why Dixie had lied to him. She was right about one thing she told him—she was getting good at lying—real good.

A door knock brought Deloris out of his melancholy but not for long. Standing at the rear of his truck was the client for whom he had drafted the summons and complaint and with whom he had signed the contingency-fee contract to sue the other party involved in their two-car accident.

"Yeah, Mr. Willis?" Deloris said, looking at his client.

Willis wore a cervical collar.

Deloris pointed to the neck brace. "You come to show me that, did you?"

"Oh, no sir. My chiropractor, he told me to git this here." Willis laughed. "Fella I run into at the post office, know what he asked me? He asked me iffen I was some kinda preacher. He was of the mind this here was something like you see them highfaluting preacher mens wear around—you know them 'Pisskapagens' and Cadillacs."

"Catholics," Deloris said.

"Huh?"

"They're called 'Catholics,' not Cadillacs. A Cadillac is a car, doncha know."

"Yes, sir. Anyhow, I told him I wasn't no preacher, and I wore this here on 'count of my neck, it'd started to smart something awful."

"Did it hurt before or after you visited the chiropractor?"

Willis' mouth dropped open. He looked at Deloris wide-eyed. "Huh?"

Deloris waved the question away. "Never mind. Whatcha want?"

Willis shuffled his feet and pulled a long envelope from a rear pocket of his blue jeans. "Well, sir, I figger I should bring you this here and see iffen you feel like it might could hurt my case a little bit."

He handed Deloris the envelope whose return address indicated it came from an automobile insurance company.

Deloris withdrew the letter from inside. One sentence in particular caught his eye. It read in part:

> We regret to inform you that your policy has lapsed because you failed to make a timely payment of the premium when it came due; therefore, you had no automobile liability coverage provided by us on the date the accident in question occurred. Please let us know if we can assist you with your insurance needs in the future.

"What 'bout it, Lawyer Meek? Whatcha think?"

Troubles and Kuddles

Deloris looked at his judgment-proof client and shook the letter. "This won't hurt you a bit. But as for me? Now, that's a far different story."

"I don't git ya."

"You wouldn't."

CHAPTER FOUR

Several days had gone by since the visit from Jade Ziglar. In the interim, Deloris had seen Dixie twice, and each time only briefly. The first encounter occurred in the office of the registrar of mesne conveyances and the second outside the Stilwell's Men Store downtown.

Deloris thought Dixie to be overly friendly both times. On each occasion, Billy Joe Pratt had accompanied her. Deloris started to ask about their visit to the Grease Pit but chickened out. One question Dixie asked outside the registrar's office was whether he had heard anything from Ginger in recent days. Before asking the question, Dixie seemed sullen but seemed to lighten up when he told her he had not had any contact with Ginger.

Deloris left Silver's Five and Dime where he ate a stuffed tomato at the lunch counter and hiked the three blocks back to his truck. A note taped to the passenger-side window asked him to come next door to Kingry's Insurance.

The moment he entered the office, a secretary hailed him. "Mr. Meek, you got a long-distance phone call about forty-five minutes ago from somebody who called herself—you won't believe this." She laughed. "Said her name was Miss Chickadee. Told me to tell you it was urgent you call her. She left a number which you can reach her at."

"Miss Chickadee, you say?" The name did not ring a bell.

"What she said."

Deloris had a revelation. "Could it have been Childree?"

The woman bit her lip and squinted. "Well, maybe. But I thought she said Chickadee. Anyway, here's the number she left. Like I say, she called long distance." She handed Deloris a pink slip.

Deloris groaned at the mention of long distance. He loathed having to pay tolls for making telephone calls, especially those he surmised would dent his pocket.

"She say anything about me reversing the charges?"

The secretary shook her head. "Nope. All she said was for you to call her at this number. I could've sworn she said her name was Ginger Chickadee though. You know, like the bird." Bringing both hands to her chest and flapping her folded arms, she laughed and chirped in a poor imitation of a songbird.

Deloris was not amused. "And she didn't say anything about maybe her calling me back later on?"

"Sure didn't."

He sighed and felt his chest tighten. "Mind if I use your phone. I'm gonna try reversing the charges anyway. If she won't accept them, then I won't talk to her."

Deloris placed the call. When Ginger answered, she surprised him by agreeing to pay for the call.

"Hello, Deloris?"

"Yeah, Ginger. Where you at?"

"In Greenfield, here in my apartment."

"In Greenfield? I thought you said you were going to Awenasa."

"I did, but Awenasa is only five miles from here."

"I see. Did you talk to Holcomb?"

"No. Funny thing, when I got Awenasa he'd vamoosed. Nobody seems to know where he went to. I heard he left behind a ton of unpaid bills—which is typical of him. He's got all kinds of people out looking for him."

"I doubt if he'll be hard to find. It's kinda hard to hide a big ol' tent."

"You want to hear the funny part? They say he not only left his tent but everything else too—his trailer, the organ, chairs, pickle jars—"

"Pickle jars?"

"Yes, pickle jars. Don't you remember he used them to collect the love offerings?"

Deloris nodded. He remembered.

"He just all of a sudden disappeared one day. He didn't tell anybody, not his tent man, his organist. Not anybody," Ginger said.

"Were the police notified?"

"I don't know. I presume they were. Process servers are out there swarming all over the place, so I was told, posting notices and everything."

"Are you calling me just to tell me he'd flown the coop?"

"Well, not entirely." After a pause, she said, "Guess who showed up yesterday, though?"

"Wally Teal."

"Yep. He told me he'd seen you, and you'd helped him. He looks real good. He wants to begin anew, get him a new dummy, and so forth. I'm letting him stay with me temporarily, but he's not here right now. He's out looking for a job, one that'll carry him over while he works on new routines and gets a new dummy made and all."

"How about you? Are you working?"

"Yes, I am. I've got a job with a bottling company, inspecting bottles. It's not much of a job and only pays minimum wage, but that's okay. I get to sit down all day. I don't plan to stay with them long."

"Sounds like you got an easy job."

"It's harder than you might think. Looking at those bottles hour after hour kind of mesmerizes you. After a while, they get to where they all look the same." Ginger laughed. "The other day I let a bottle get by me which had five Popsicle sticks in it. Can you believe that? Five Popsicle sticks. Fortunately, the production manager caught it before the drink got capped. He brought it over to show me. He told me it had enough lumber in it to build a house."

Deloris chuckled. "Had the bottle gotten by y'all, it could've made some lawyer rich, doncha know." He switched the phone from one ear to the other. "Where's Wally looking?"

"Anywhere and everywhere. He doesn't care. He just wants a job. If he doesn't find anything soon, I maybe can get him on down at the plant, separating bottles, operating the fork lift—feeding the bottle washer. They're always looking for somebody, seems like. Maybe he could be a route salesman. He relates to people well, and the pay's pretty good—lot better than we get paid there in the plant."

"How come you're not at work right now?"

"Why? They're replacing the thingamajig which puts carbonated water in the bottles. They told me to take the day off. So, that's what I'm doing. I'd enjoy it, but I'm not being paid anything."

Deloris put his hand over the telephone mouthpiece and coughed. "Oh, while I'm thinking about it, when you see him, tell Wally this Yankee-talking fella came by my office a few days ago, looking for him. Told me his name was Jade Ziglar."

"Jade Ziglar?"

He wanted to know if I might know where Wally was. I told him he might try going to Awenasa where you are. I told him Wally was looking for you."

"Jade Ziglar, you say?"

"Yeah. Jade Ziglar. Look here, you haven't said why you telephoned me other than to tell me about Wally."

"Silly me. I should've told you my good news right off. A local UHF TV station here in Greenfield heard about me. My guess is the owner of the plant may've told them I was working here. He's a real nice man, Mr. Everett is. Anyway, he knows all about my background and everything. The station wants me to do a kid's show for them in the late afternoon, starting in a couple of months, which is good because it'll give me time to get me another dummy made and practice with it, and, you know, work on a personality for it, decide on its name and all. So, it's good Wally showed up when he did. Maybe he can help me with it and everything. We might could even do the show together. I don't know. I'd have to discuss it with the program director. Anyway, they sent me a proposed contract for a show that'll only run for a trial period— three months is all. I don't feel like signing it until I've had a lawyer look it over, and you're the only lawyer I know. Would you do that for me?" She paused a moment. "Pretty please."

Deloris did not respond right off. Some lawyers stay away from criminal law, others from tort law or still others from labor law or property law or other fields. Because of his earlier academic problems with the law of contracts both in law school and with the bar examination, Deloris made every effort to avoid having anything to do with contract law, a well-nigh impossible undertaking for any lawyer as a practical matter. Lawyers cannot avoid contracts and the law and problems associated with them no matter what. They bloom all over, in insurance policies, settlement agreements, trade deals, attorney fee arrangements—everywhere two or more persons gather to engage in some kind of transaction and there is conflict or the possibility of conflict.

"You sure you want me to do it?" Deloris said, his voice tinged with hesitation. "Last time I tried to do something for you, things, they didn't exactly turn out too good for you, doncha know."

"I don't blame you, Mr. Meek. You couldn't help that ol' mean judge choosing to believe Brother Holcomb instead of me. Can I mail you the contract or should I try to get some other lawyer to review it?"

An empty feeling engulfed Deloris. "Well, yeah, send it on. But I'll tell you, I'm far from being an expert on these things."

Deloris started to tell her goodbye, but a question popped into his mind. "Oh, let me ask you something before you hang up."

"Yes."

"Speaking of Kuddles."

"What about her?"

"Did Brother Holcomb leave her behind too?"

"No," Ginger said, sounding sad. "Wherever he disappeared to, you can bet your life she's with him. Poor little thing."

***

Once off the telephone, Deloris hurried back to his office to meet with Root Johnson and his brother Cab. The Johnson brothers had left word at Kingry's Insurance they wanted to meet with him.

Deloris met the two men at the rear of his truck and invited them inside. Once they entered, Deloris immediately regretted his decision. Both men emitted a strong, eye-watering body odor. Had he caught a whiff of their stench when he met them outside, he never would have invited them into his office. He resolved to make the interview a fast one, if possible, for more reason than their bad

Troubles and Kuddles

smell. He doubted whether either of them carried so much as a half-dollar in his pocket.

Deloris studied the brothers as they sat in front of his desk. The two men, dressed in blue overalls and scuffed, heel-worn brogan boots, sat smiling at him through missing teeth, a baseball cap in each one's lap and each one's hands tucked inside the bib to his overalls. One ball cap advertised a popular beer while the other read "Cocks."

"So, what's y'all's problem?" Deloris asked.

"Tell him, Root," one brother said.

"Okay. I'm Root, and this here is my brother Cab. I'm the oldest."

Deloris removed a fountain pen from his shirt pocket and wrote down both names. "Okay. And why you fellas wanna talk to me for?"

"On 'count we up and got ourselves 'rested here in town near 'bout two months back and they told us our trial, it was fixin' to come up. We figgered we might need us a lawyer, and we heard tell of you, sir."

"And just why were you arrested?"

" 'Cause they said we bought us some whiskey what didn't have no stamps on it."

"And both of you claim you're innocent, I take it?" Deloris said, his eyes narrowed and making no attempt not to sound incredulous.

"Yes, sir," both men said at once.

"Innocent as a new-born baby lamb," Cab added.

"Uh-huh. Let me ask you this. Did you buy some whiskey from somebody?"

"No, sir. We ain't done that. No siree. We—"

"When you got arrested, did you have some whiskey on you?"

"Oh, yes sir. We shore did. Two half-pints."

"But you didn't buy it."

"No, sir. It was give to us," Root said.

"And the man what give it to us, he's the same one what 'rested us," Cab said. "He told us he was a ABC, which we didn't have no idea what it was at the time, did we Root?"

"Shore didn't."

Deloris tilted his head to the side. "Let me get this straight. The arresting officer, an ABC officer, gave you the whiskey."

"Yes, sir."

"In other words, y'all didn't buy anything from the arresting officer, right?

"No, sir," both men answered.

"Lord's my witness," added Root, a hand held high.

"Mine too," echoed Cab. "Ain't neither one of us been taught to story, Lawyer Meek. Mama, God rest her soul, she raised us better'n that."

"She shore did," Root confirmed

Deloris leaned forward in his chair. "Yeah? How about this. Tell me from the beginning how all this happened?" He raised his pen, preparing to take notes.

Root closed his eyes and stroked the stubble on his chin. "Well, Lawyer Meek, it happened thisaway," he said, his black eyes now open and shifting right and left. "You see here, me and Cab, we come to town to visit our older brother Okie, and me and Cab, we wound up goin' to a revival meetin' with him and his wife Sara Nell there at Mount Olive Free-Will Baptist. After church got done with, we was 'posed to meet him and Sara Nell at Grubb's for some apple pie and 'nilla ice cream. You know, they got the bestist in the world there."

"Uh-huh," Deloris said. "So y'all had been to church. And what night was this?"

The brothers looked at each other. They both spoke at the same time.

"Friday," said one.

"Saturday," said the other.

Already Deloris didn't believe a word either brother said or would say. He surmised the only time the Johnsons had ever been inside a church was to perform manual labor of some kind or to escape the elements, if then even.

"Okay, let's just say it was one night right before the weekend," Deloris said, tongue in cheek.

"Yes, sir," Root said. "I don't reckon it matters noways what night it was, does it? One night's pretty much like all the rest of them, ain't they?"

"Before you go on, where y'all from?"

" 'Bout halfway 'twixt here and Greenfield."

"I see. Go on, Root," Deloris said, his pen poised to continue writing.

Root nodded and smiled at Cab. "Wellsir, as me and him was headin' down Line Street, this fella, he come out from 'twix them two buildin's they got there by the railroad tracks on South Main—you know, where the oyster bar and hardware store are, and he said to us, real nice like, 'Hey, you two fellas, y'all wait up a sec. Y'all don't want no free whiskey, I bet?' Cab, he said, 'What'd you say?' And the man, who ain't neither one of us never seen afore, he asked us again iffen we didn't want no free whiskey. Why, what man wouldn't want no free whiskey, huh? 'Specially somebody like me and Cab, both us tired as a couple of Tennessee coonhounds come daylight. 'Fore we'd gone to church that night, we'd been helpin' Eugene Slocomb clear out a lot downtown where he figgers on putting him in a used-car business. That church service, it took a lot outta both us, what with all the singin' and clappin' and all."

"And me with this sore shoulder I got," Cab interjected. "Using that sling blade didn't help it none."

"Your sore shoulder, it ain't nothin'. I got me a sore back," Root said. "That's a whole lot worser than any ol' shoulder hurtin'."

"No, it ain't neither," Cab said. He rolled his shoulder, "When I do it this here way, it still—"

Deloris held up an open hand. "Look here, y'all, I don't have time to referee some kinda hurting contest. All I wanna know about is y'all's arrest."

"Yes, sir," Root said. "It was like this here. Me and Cab, we both told him 'Yes, sir, we wouldn't mind iffen we did have some free whiskey, that is, iffen you've got some and it's free, shore nuff.' " He turned to Cab. "Ain't that what we said?"

"That's what we said, all right. Lord's my witness. We ain't had no money for no whiskey. We'd give all we had to the church—every penny."

"Say you did?" Deloris said, dipping his head and making a face.

Root continued. "Anyways, the man said, 'Well, here's a bottle for each one of y'all.' And he give us each one a half-pint, free of charge. When me and Cab went to thank him, he said, 'I gotcha now, by cracky, and I 'rest y'all in the name of the law for buyin' unstamped whiskey,' which we ain't neither one done, Lawyer Meek. Like I say, he give it to us and didn't ask us for no money or nothin', and we didn't pay him nothin', did we, Cab?"

"Not one cent," Cab answered. "Like I said, we ain't had none to pay him with."

Deloris settled back in his chair and folded his arms across his chest. "Just so I can understand, you two were headed down the street here in town one Friday or Saturday night."

"Yes, sir," Root said. "And we were both 'bout give out."

"Y'all were just walking along, minding your own business, not bothering anybody, and a man who didn't neither one of you know comes out from between two buildings and offers each of y'all a free bottle of whiskey. You tell him you'd like to have it, he gives it to you—outta the goodness of his heart, I suppose—and then he arrests you both. Do I have it right?"

Root slapped his thigh. "You shore do. It happened 'xactly like that, Lawyer Meek."

"Shore did," Cab said, nodding. "Lord's my witness."

Deloris dropped his arms into his lap and bent forward. "Y'all say y'all were coming from church?"

Both men nodded.

"On our way to git some apple pie and ice cream," Root said.

"And meet our brother Okie," said Cab.

"Don't forget Sara Nell," said Root.

Troubles and Kuddles

Deloris cocked his head. "Let me ask you fellas this. What'd the preacher preach on? Can either of y'all tell me? What about it, Cab?"

Cab scratched the top of his head. "I can't recollect. You 'member, Root?"

"Somethin' 'bout Jesus, think it was," Root said. "I know the preacher mentioned his name a time or two."

After a brief pause, Deloris pitched forward in his chair. "And how'd y'all find out about me?"

Cab smiled. "Root, tell Lawyer Meek how we come to hear 'bout him."

"You mean tell him 'bout the fella at the jail."

"Yeah. Go on. Tell him."

"You tell him."

"Okay," Cab said, sounding somewhat aggravated. "We met this fella in the jailhouse and told him 'bout what'd happened and all. When we said somethin' 'bout goin' to church, he said one Sunday evenin' at his church the preacher, he was quotatin' scripture, talkin' about hellfire, worms, and all kinda torments they got down there in hell for sinners, and how sin'll cause you all kinda trouble, and—"

Root interrupted. "It was right 'bout then, the fella in the jail told us, the reverend stopped his preachin' and looked the crowd over and said somethin' like, 'And who you gonna call on iffen you git yourself in a whole buncha trouble?' This woman what he said was sittin' in a wheelchair down there in front, she hollered out, "Iffen it was me, Preacher, I'd call Lawyer Deloris Meek, Esquire and Notary Public."

Cab crossed his arms and nodded, a pleased look on his face. "And that's how we knowed to come see you, sir. Iffen you was good 'nough for a Christian woman saddled in a wheelchair, then we figgered you was good 'nough for us."

A brief silence followed.

"Let me ask you fellas this," Deloris said. "What kinda work do y'all do when you're not clearing lots?"

"Me and him? Pulp wood mostly. You know, cut it," Root said. "And when we ain't doin' that, we sometime hire on as grease monkeys at this here fillin' station out on Belle's Highway, fixin' flat tires, pumpin' gas—stuff like that—changin' oil, lube'catin' cars and trucks. It's close to where we live at."

"Tell y'all what," Deloris said.

Both men sat up straight in his chair and put a hand to an ear.

"If I take your case, it'll cost you three hundred dollars, and I'll take care of your fine."

Each brother's mouth dropped open. "But Lawyer Meek, we ain't got no three hundred dollars," Root said, dropping his head.

"No, sir, we don't," Cab added. "Looky here." He stood and jerked out both side-pockets of his overalls.

Deloris stood and stepped from behind his desk and eased over to the back door. "My advice, fellas, is for y'all to go before the magistrate all by yourselves and plead guilty. The fine's not but a hundred dollars each, and he'll probably cut it to fifty if you act like you're really, really sorry. If I were to go with you, I'd have to charge you a little something for my time, and there's no point in y'all taking on that expense." He opened the door. "So, good morning, fellas, and good luck. Really, I'm doing you a favor."

The would-be clients prepared to leave.

Root stood and put his baseball hat on. He looked at Cab and nodded. Cab hauled himself to his feet and placed his hat back on as well. Both men joined Deloris at the door, but not before engaging in whispered conversation out of Deloris' hearing.

"Wellsir, Lawyer Meek, me and Cab, we both done thought 'bout what you said do."

"Yes, sir," Cab said. "We in agreement. What you told us while ago, it makes a heappa sense."

"But afore we mosey on, Lawyer Meek," Root said, "can I ask you somethin' other? I'm kinda curious. How come you got you a girl's name?"

Deloris laughed. "Oh, it's not a girl's name. I spell it with an 'i.'"

"Say you do?" Root said, scratching his cheek.

"And since you asked me about my name," Deloris said, "how'd y'all get the names 'Root' and 'Cab'?"

Root smiled. "Mama, she named all us young'uns after stuff she liked to eat. My real name is 'Rutabaga.'" He angled his head toward his brother. "Hisen's 'Cabbage.' We got us a younger brother named 'Turnip.' Everybody, they call him 'Nip.'"

"Any sisters?" Deloris asked, fanning the air to ward off their stink.

"Yes, sir. Two," Root said, "'Peanut' and 'Lemon,' only we call her 'Sweetie Lemon.'"

"How about Okie?" Deloris asked. "I'm guessing his name is Okra?"

Root smiled. "Yes, sir, you hit the nail on the head. But one more thing, Lawyer Meek, afore we head out. Us talkin' 'bout vegetables 'minded me of it."

"Yeah?"

"Me and Cab, we think we might have us a real good lawsuit 'gainst a supermarket store. You might wanna handle it. Might make us all three rich."

Deloris sat up straight. His interest in the Johnson brothers had all of a sudden risen. "Say you do? Which one?"

"One down on South Main, the Nickel Jamboree."

"One of you slip and fall or something?"

Root shook his head. "No, sir. What happened was this. Sometime back, me and Cab, we bought us a watermelon, and once we brung it on home and cut it open, guess what? It was all rotten on the inside. It was all yellow—yellow as a summer squash. So, we chunked it. Whoever heard of a watermelon what's got yellow meat? I know I ain't."

"Me neither," Cab added.

"That store, it gypped us, that's what they done, all right. Didn't they Cab?"

"They shore did," Cab responded. "Beat us outta thirty-five cents. We ain't spendin' no more our hard-earned money in there no more, tell you that."

"Right," Root said. "We shore ain't." He squinted at Deloris. "Think we might have us a case, Lawyer Meek?"

Deloris smiled and leaned his head to the side. "Tell you what, gentlemen. Why don't y'all go see Lawyer Oleander Chiselbrook. That's his kinda case. He specializes in watermelon cases from what I hear."

"Ain't he the one they call 'Mr. Smudge'?"

Deloris nodded. "But I don't know about the 'mister' part."

"Where can we find his office at?" Root asked.

"Next door to Ins and Outs Bail Bonding Company. You know, across from the jailhouse."

"Yeah, we know where that is, don't we Cab? It's the one Daddy and Uncle Jack used most times. We started to use them our ownselves when we got throwed in jail but didn't do it. Dunno why we didn't do it. You, Cab?"

"I don't think we was all that anxious to git out, tired as we was and them feedin' us good like they was doin'. Later on, the jailor, he give us this card of them other'n, and we hooked up with them."

Deloris angled his head toward the open door. "Okay, well, y'all check with Mr. Smudge."

Both men tipped their hats. "Much obliged, Lawyer Meek. Shore been nice talkin' to you," Cab said.

As he held the door open for the two men to pass through, Deloris received a surprise. Dixie St. John stood in the parking lot, facing them, her arms crossed and her foot tapping.

***

Dixie closed her eyes and held her nose as Root and Cab walked by, grinning and snickering and elbowing each other. She turned and watched them as they left the parking lot. "They some of your kinfolk, Deloris?" she said, facing him once again.

"No, uh-huh. Shoppers, which I seem to get a lot of. But you can't never tell what . . ."

Dixie stepped into the truck. "I wish you'd get you a regular office." She sniffed the air. "Gracious me, that awful smell . . ."

"You talking about those two fellas who just left here?" Deloris said, laughing. "That's Rutabaga and Cabbage. Their last name's Johnson."

Troubles and Kuddles

"Rutabaga and Cabbage Johnson? And I thought you had a funny name," Dixie said, waving a hand in front of her face. "Whew."

"If you wanna, we can go stand outside until this smell goes away—if it ever does."

"You better hope it does or you'll need to get you a new truck. Whewee! You got any Vicks VapoRub?"

"For what?"

"Put up my nose. It'd help me deal with that smell. I bet it's already gotten into all your clothes and on your furniture and everything. How could you stand being in here with them with the doors all closed?"

"I don't have any Vicks, but will it really do the trick?"

"Works for me."

Deloris and Dixie stepped outside and stood in a sunny spot near the front of his truck.

"You surprised me by coming here, doncha know," Deloris said. "Billy Joe send you?"

"No, I took off."

"He let you off?"

"No, I took it off." She cupped her hand on the back of her neck. "What's he gonna do, fire me? I don't think so."

"Whatcha want, if he didn't send you?" he asked. His voice had an urgency about it.

Deloris ducked her head. "I ran into Glory Hiers this morning. She was coming out of the bank. She said she hasn't seen me since Billy Joe and I came to the Grease Pit and bought some pie after, as she put it, 'you and him come from the picture show.' She said she happened to tell you about us being there together."

Deloris' shoulders drooped. "Yeah, she mentioned it. To be honest, what she said did kinda throw me since I thought you'd told me you'd gone to the movies with your mama. But it ain't none of my business, now is it?"

Dixie put a hand to her hip. "Well, I had gone to the picture show with Mama. I happened to go to the Grease Pit later on at the same time Billy Joe just happened to come there. While I went inside, Mama waited in the car. I simply ran in to get two slices of pie, one for me and one for Mama. That's all there was to it. We didn't go there together, he and I."

Deloris stood staring at her, rolling his tongue against his cheek. "Why you telling me all this?"

"Because I wanted you to know what happened, that's all," she said in a huff. "I don't want you getting any funny ideas."

He shrugged. "Well, okay. Whatever."

Neither spoke for a moment or two. "Tell me this, Deloris. Is your invitation to go to the passion pit, is it still open?"

He turned his head to the side and looked at her out of the corner of his eye. "Passion pit?"

"You know, the drive-in theater."

"Oh," he said with a laugh. "Yeah. Why?"

"Let's go tonight. Do you wanna?"

"Are you serious?" he said in disbelief

"Why certainly I am. I don't kid around."

He slapped his thigh with delight as his mind jumped ahead to being alone with one of the most beautiful creatures God ever made in a motor vehicle parked in a darkened area. "Then we'll do it, by George."

"Great! I'll drive Mama's car." She pointed to his truck. "I doubt if they'd let us in the place with you driving that thing there."

"That's okay with me," he said, smiling.

"One more thing."

"What?"

"Mind if I bring Mama? After all, it's her car. She and I'll sit in the front. That way, you can have the whole back seat all to yourself so you can spread out."

CHAPTER FIVE

It was after ten p.m. and raining when Deloris left a board of directors meeting of the local Elks Lodge where he served as a trustee. About all the meeting accomplished was the approval of a contract to repair the roof of the lodge. Most of the discussion centered on military veterans and plans for an upcoming initiation ceremony.

He never understood why his brother Elks wanted him on the board. He was not a veteran, he did not play golf or tennis, and he never married. Like all his lodge brethren, he was a white male over the age of twenty-one who believed in God—well, sorta did—and did not sympathize with Bolsheviks, anarchists, or I.W.W. members. The only reason he could give for his selection was the "herd," as Deloris referred to his fellow Elks, must have wanted a trustee who they thought knew a little something about contracts, being he was a lawyer. If this is what they had in mind when they placed him on the board, they got exactly what they wanted. When it came to contract law, "a little" was about all he knew.

Deloris parked his truck in front of the small, white, asbestos-siding house he rented in a low-rent section of town. He decided to stay in the truck and wait until the rain slackened before making a run for his front door. Deloris rested his head against the driver-side window and closed his eyes as he listened to the sounds of the wind blowing and the rain pelting the glass and metal of his truck. These sounds would have lulled him asleep had the rain not subsided minutes later.

Once the rain became a light sprinkle, he jumped from the truck onto the street and made a dash for the front stoop some ten yards away. As he opened the screen door, he picked up the afternoon newspaper behind it, thankful for a paperboy who had the presence of mind to protect the paper from the weather conditions. After he stepped inside and turned on a light, he glanced at the front page of the paper. His eyes fell upon a heading in the lower left-hand corner of the page. It read: *Shot Fired at Revivalist Jimmy Holcomb.*

Two things about the news article surprised him. One, Holcomb had returned to Awenasa; and two, somebody apparently disliked him enough to take aim at him.

The brief story accompanying the headline reported someone had fired at Holcomb while he lunched with his ventriloquist dummy at a roadside picnic area near Awenasa. In his haste to flee the area, he sped away in his car, leaving the dummy behind. When Holcomb drove back to retrieve the dummy, he found it gone. The sheriff claimed his investigation had uncovered "a person of interest." He refused to identify that individual.

Deloris thought of Ginger but immediately dismissed the thought.

No sooner had he laid the paper aside than he heard his telephone ring. He hurried through the living room into the hallway to answer it.

"Hello," he said.

"Mr. Meek?"

He recognized the voice on the other end. "Ginger?"

"Yes, it's me. Have you heard about what happened to Brother Holcomb? It's all over the news up here."

"I just this minute read about it. About all the paper said was somebody took a shot at him somewhere near Awenasa."

"Oh, Mr. Meek . . ."

Ginger began sobbing.

Deloris listened for a moment. "Ginger. Ginger," he said when he decided he had endured enough of her crying, "what's the matter? Hush with all that now."

The crying became less but a sniffling followed.

"Okay, now tell me what's got you all upset."

"I'm sorry," she said between sniffs. "I guess it's because the paper said something about the police having what they called a 'person' of interest,' and I'm scared it may be me."

He heard a couple more sniffs.

"Now, why you think that, Ginger?"

"Why?" She did not respond immediately.

"Yeah, why? What reason would they have to suspect you?"

"The lawsuit I brought that time. They might think I shot at him because I—"

"Nonsense. You only sued him, Ginger. You didn't try to kill him. You did what any right-minded citizen would do under the same circumstances. You went to the law. So, don't worry about doing this. All that's pretty much water under the bridge now. It's history. Another thing, the paper said it happened around lunchtime near Awenasa, and you'd be in Greenfield at that time miles away, either going on your lunch break or just about ready to go on it there at the bottling plant."

"Okay," Ginger said after a brief pause, "but could I ask you something else, Mr. Meek?"

His stomach tightened. "Sure," he said through gritted teeth. He did not want anything more to do with Ginger, Kuddles, and the Reverend Holcomb. Ever since he and Ginger met, it seemed trouble shadowed their relationship. He rubbed his head in remembrance of the beating he got at the Louisiana nightclub when he went there to catch her and Wally's act.

"What if they come and want to ask me some questions. Should I talk to them?"

"Them? The police, you mean? Why shouldn't you talk to them? You don't have nothing to hide, do you?"

Ginger did not answer.

"I asked you whether you've got something to hide. Do you, Ginger?" his voice accusatory.

Ginger hesitated. "I don't believe . . . no, huh-uh."

"Then, I can't see any harm in you doing it. Like I say, you don't have nothing to hide. If you don't talk to them, however, they'll think you are trying to hide something, doncha see. Like I said a while ago, you've got a good alibi. You were at work in Greenfield or gone on your lunch break there."

"Okay," she said after a pause, "if you feel it's all right."

"Ginger, is Wally there with you?"

"No," she said, still sniffling. "He's gone to work."

"Work? He's got him a job already?"

"Yes, at the hospital—as an orderly. He's done that kind of work before. Why? You need him for something? He works from eleven p.m. to seven a.m. five days a week. I might could try to reach him for you."

"No, I don't need him; I was just wondering where he was, particularly since you're so upset. You sound like you need somebody with you right now is all."

The sniffling stopped, followed by a brief silence. "Okay, Mr. Meek. Thank you. Can I call you again should I look like I might need you? Would that be all right?"

Again, his stomach tensed. "Of course. Now, get a grip on yourself and go to bed. That's what I'm gonna do after I watch the late news. Goodnight, Ginger."

About ten minutes later, Deloris' phone rang once more. Again, the caller was Ginger.

Deloris swore to himself. "What now, Ginger?"

"Mr. Meek, I've got a confession to make."

"What?" He braced himself for bad news.

"I wasn't exactly honest with you a few minutes ago."

Ginger's withholding of information from Deloris did not surprise him. He had practiced law long enough to know clients often failed to disclose everything their counsel needed to be aware of to provide proper representation.

"Whatcha mean you weren't exactly honest with me?"

Oh, Mr. Meek . . ." A sudden bawling overtook her words.

Deloris removed the phone from his ear and shook his head before returning it. "Come on now. Hush crying and tell me what's wrong."

"Well, okay. But you're going to get upset with me. I know you will be."

"Tell me anyway." He braced himself for what he suspected would be bad news.

"Early this yesterday morning, I received a telephone call from Jimmy."

"Jimmy?"

"Brother Holcomb"

"Oh. How'd he know how to get in touch with you?"

"I don't know."

"So what'd Holcomb say?"

"He said he was coming back to Awenasa and wanted me to meet him at a roadside picnic area right outside of town on Belle's Highway a little after noon. He said he wanted to discuss Kuddles with me and maybe our getting back together. He apologized for our past difficulties, saying the Devil had gotten a hold on him and made him do all sorts of bad things, including running off like he'd did, leaving people holding the bag. He said he wanted to make everything right between us and with everybody else too.

"To make a long story short, I borrowed a friend's car and drove out there to meet him. I felt sorry for him, he sounded so pitiful over the phone. But when I got to the picnic area, guess what? He wasn't anywhere to be seen. For a moment, I thought maybe I'd had gotten the wrong picnic area, but that's when I saw Kuddles. She was just sitting there on a bench at one of the back tables, big as you please. She had on real dirty clothes, like he'd not been taking very good care of her. My heart just went out to the poor little—"

Deloris cut her off. "So what'd you do?"

"What'd I do? I waited around for about ten or fifteen minutes, and when he didn't show, I put Kuddles in the car, and came on back to town. I thought by his leaving Kuddles like he did it was his way of apologizing to me—you know, atoning for everything he'd put me through. When I got back to town, I went on back to work like usual. Tell you one thing, it was hard inspecting bottles. I kept crying, I was so happy to have Kuddles back with me. I couldn't wait to tell Wally."

"So you didn't see Holcomb anywhere when you got to the roadside park?"

"No."

"See anybody?"

"No."

She paused a moment. Deloris thought he heard her blow her nose.

"Mr. Meek, do you still feel like I can talk to the police if they come here? I'm awfully worried. I got sense enough to know this doesn't look good. You know with me having sued him and having Kuddles here with me after all that happened. I know now I shouldn't have taken her."

"Why didn't you tell me all this to start with?"

"I was too scared to."

"Well, from what you told me, that changes everything. My gut reaction is tell you not to say anything to them, at least not until you have a lawyer present." Deloris had a sudden thought. "Ginger, you don't own a gun, do you?"

"Oh, heavens no."

"Okay. Good. Well, try not to worry. If they had wanted to question you, they'd probably done done it by now. Try and get you some sleep. Call me if you need me. Goodnight."

***

A ringing telephone against a clap of thunder awakened Deloris. He flipped over onto his other side and checked the alarm clock on the nightstand. It read seven forty-five a.m. He swore to himself. He had intended to sleep until at least eight and, since it was raining, perhaps even longer. The phone continued to ring. Yawning, he lifted the phone off its cradle.

"Hello," he said with a not-too-friendly voice.

"Mr. Meek?"

Deloris shook himself further awake. "Yeah, this is him. Who's this?"

"It's me, Wally."

"Wally?"

"Yes, sir. Wally Teal. I'm sorry. I had to call you."

"Had to call me?"

"Yes, sir. Ginger's gone missing."

"Gone missing? I just talked to her last night—right before the eleven o'clock news came on. She was fixing to go to bed I thought."

"Did you know she's letting me room here with her until I can find me a place?"

"Yeah, she told me."

"I got me a job working the graveyard shift at the hospital as an orderly."

"Yeah, she told me that too."

Troubles and Kuddles

"Anyhow, I finished my shift about a half hour ago, and when I came back here, I saw the door to her bedroom was open, and I could see she wasn't in her bed. I looked for her in the kitchen and bathroom, but she wasn't in either place. I don't think she went out for an early morning walk because it's raining cats and dogs up here."

"Mmmhuh. It's raining here too."

"I got a little worried and decided to call you. I found your number written on her phone book."

"So, what you want from me?" Deloris yawned again.

"Should I call the police or something? It's not like her to not be here at this time of morning. She never did anything like this when we worked together before. When I spoke with her last night before I left for work, she said she'd heard about Mr. Holcomb on the radio being shot at. She said she might try and contract you. Did she say anything about going any place after she talked with you, sir?"

"No, but she's not in the habit of clearing her goings and comings with me, Wally. But if it'll make you feel any better, why doncha call the police if she doesn't show back up, say in about an hour or so. I'm sure she's all right."

"Okay. I think I might call them soon as I hang up."

"Whatever. Goodnight, Wally, or rather, good morning."

"Oh, Mr. Meek?"

"Huh?"

"I just now noticed something."

"What?"

"Kuddles is not here. I suppose Ginger told you Holcomb left her at this roadside picnic area and Ginger brought her back to her apartment this evening after she got off work, didn't she?"

"Yes, she did."

"You suppose Ginger's trying to hide Kuddles some place, just in case the police should come looking for her?"

"Wally, I have no idea. I would certainly hope not. When she comes back and, if she's done that, you tell her to bring Kuddles back to her apartment immediately and contact the police and tell them how she happened to have Kuddles in her possession."

"Yes, sir."

Deloris hung up the phone and went back to sleep. His venture into the marvelous and sometimes terrifying world of dreams, however, lasted only a little while. The telephone awoke him again.

"Wally," Deloris said, "what is—"

A female voice interrupted. "Deloris, it's me, Ginger."

Deloris shook himself more awake. "Ginger, what the heck's going on? First, Wally calls me and now you. Next thing you know, I'll be hearing from Kuddles."

A brief silence followed.

"I'm in jail, Deloris," Ginger said sobbing. "They—"

Deloris sat up in bed "In jail, you say? What the—"

"They've charged me with robbery and assault to kill or something like that. The police arrested me after they came to my house and found Kuddles."

"Found Kuddles?"

"Yes, I had her sitting on my sofa. Oh, Deloris, can you come help me, come get me out of jail? This place is awful. I'm scared to death."

CHAPTER SIX

After the telephone rang four times, Dixie St. John answered Deloris' call. Gum smacks punctuated her tiresome voice. "Law office. And before you ask, no, he's not in and I don't know when he will be."

Deloris had watched Dixie chew gum before. Notwithstanding her great beauty, whenever she chewed gum, which was often, the way she did it reminded him of how a cow ate—the mouth moved from side to side. Apart from that, he had anticipated Billy Joe would answer the phone and not Dixie. She seldom made it to work on time, at least according to Billy Joe.

"Dixie, you say Billy Joe's not around?"

"Nope. Whenever I'm early, like this morning, he's late."

"When are you ever early?"

"Any time I beat him here to the office, and today, it's one of them days."

"But it's almost a quarter to eleven."

"So?"

"You got any idea where he might be right now? I tried his home phone. I kinda need to talk to him. I need his help."

"Will you ever learn?"

"Do you know where he is or not?" Deloris said, his impatience showing through.

"My, aren't we testy this morning. If I had to guess, he's down at police court trying to get the jump on the deadbeats before Smudge Chiselbrook can grab hold of them and beat the poor devils out of what little money they've got squirreled away."

"Thanks. I'll head over there."

"What do you need him for?"

Deloris ignored her question and hung up the phone. He hurried out of the insurance office, hoping he would find Billy Joe in the municipal courtroom at City Hall.

A few minutes later and a couple of blocks away, Deloris arrived at the City Hall. He spotted Billy Joe upon entering the courtroom, a gloomy, odorous area with walls of pale paint and peeling plaster, windows of cracked glass and grimy sashes, and rows of abused pews and filthy floors of missing tiles.

Billy Joe sat on the front row by a well-dressed, nice-looking man—too well-dressed and too nice-looking for police court, Deloris thought. Chiselbrook stood leaning against a side wall near the front, whispering and gesturing to a man with glassy eyes and dressed in coveralls. Billy Joe guessed him to be a house painter, judging from his white, paint-splashed uniform.

"All right, Mr. Pratt," said the judge, motioning Billy Joe to come forward. "I'm ready, if you are, sir." The judge turned toward Chiselbrook. "How 'bout holding it down over there, Smudge."

Smudge pointed to his ear. "Sorry, Your Honor, but 'Rembrandt' here, he can't hear too good. Claims he's got busted eardrums, but if you ask me his ears, they're kinda like my wife's kitchen floor. You know, got waxy buildup."

The judge joined the courtroom audience in laughter and waved Smudge away. "Take him out into the hall. Y'all are talking too loud." The judge faced Billy Joe and his companion as the two approached the bench and Chiselbrook and "Rembrandt" exited the courtroom.

"You represent this gentleman, Mr. Pratt?"

"Yes, sir. This is George Washington, D.C."

"Say what now?" The judge's eyes widened. "His last name is 'Washington, D.C.'?"

Pratt laughed. "Oh, no, sir. His last name is 'Washington.' I'm sorry. The D.C., that's his medical degree. He's a chiropractor—a board-certified doctor of chiropractic, in fact."

"Board? What board?"

"I dunno which one. I reckon, you know, it's the one which certifies them. His office is on Central Avenue. It's got a big ol' stainless-steel spinal column out front. I bet that thing's twenty-foot high, whatcha wanna bet. Durnest thing." He laughs. "You seen it, Judge."

"I'm familiar with it, yes."

"Have you ever seen it during Christmas? He decorates it with colored lights and a big twinkling star at the top of it. I call it a 'Christmas Spine.' "

While Pratt laughed at his own joke, no one else did.

The judge opened a file folder and studied its contents for a moment. He removed his glasses. "Mr. Washington—"

Pratt interrupted. "Huh-uh, Your Honor. It's 'Doctor.' 'Dr. Washington,' not Mr. Washington."

The judge frowned. "Okay. Excuse me, Doctor. How's that, Mr. Chiselbrook?"

Smudge smiled. "Just fine, sir." He nudged his client with his elbow.

The doctor's head bobbed.

"According to what I have here," the judge said, "you are charged with practicing veterinary medicine without a license. The affidavit says you claimed chiropractic principles could be used to treat animals, and you treated a basset hound using chiropractic principles. How do you plead, sir?"

"Your Honor," Pratt said, "my client pleads not guilty, and he wants a jury trial by his peers. He's licensed to practice chiropractic. Nothing in the law says he can't treat animals. If it did, he couldn't treat me and you, Your Honor. We're animals too, you know. They say we're descended from apes."

The judge smiled. "Well, maybe you are, sir. I'm not. Tell you what, Mr. Pratt, if Mr. Washington, I mean, Dr. Washington, will promise not to do that anymore—treat animals—I'll dismiss the charge. I'm talking about the lower animals, you know, cats, dogs, and so forth—horses, cows, wampus cats. What about it?"

"Did you say wampus cats, sir? I don't know if—"

"Yes, wampus cats. Goats, sheep, squirrels, coons, rabbits. The whole bunch. Orangutans, grasshoppers, centipedes, snakes, giraffes."

"Grasshoppers, centipedes, and snakes too, Your Honor?"

"Yep. Them too."

Pratt held a whispered conference with the chiropractor. At its conclusion, Pratt looked at the judge and smiled. "You gotta deal, Judge. No more veterinary chiropractic practice. He's only done it this one time anyhow. He's got a soft heart. He feels for the animals. That's because when he was a little boy, this big ol' truck come speeding down the street in front of his house and his precious little puppy Peedee, it run—"

"Okay, based on what you've told me, case dismissed," the judge announced.

"Much obliged, Judge. But, Your Honor, I have to tell you this." He laughed. "Dr. Washington, know what he told me? He told me the dog's owner, she came by his office last evening with the dog and said she hadn't ever seen it so happy. Said it was walking and running around, wagging its tail, like nothing had ever been wrong with it, and every time they passed by his office with that big ol' spinal column out front of it, that dog'd bark its little head off." He slapped his client on the back. "Have to tell you this, sir. If we'd gone to trial, I'd planned to introduce the dog and take everybody out to Dr. Washington's office and let everybody watch the dog react to the spinal column. You know, let you see for yourself how it'd do."

The judge rubbed his chin. "It ran around like nothing had been wrong with it, you say?" He stood and motioned for Billy Joe to come close.

Billy Joe stepped forward as the judge leaned down from the bench. The two men held a brief, whispered conversation. Once it ended, Billy Joe eased backward and spoke to his client in a soft voice. The client smiled and nodded at the judge.

The judge returned the smile and announced he would be taking a ten-minute recess.

Deloris followed Billy Joe and his client out of the courtroom, passing Smudge and his painter-client as they elbowed their way back inside.

Deloris called after Billy Joe. "Oh, Billy Joe. Got a second I need to discuss something with you."

Billy Joe turned around and, on seeing Deloris, his shoulders dropped. "Excuse me, Dr. Washington. Wait for me outside. I'll join you in a minute and give you his address. Okay?"

The doctor nodded and walked away.

"Well, now what?" Billy Joe said, frowning.

"What'd the judge want with you a while ago?" Deloris asked.

Billy Joe snorted. "You'd never guess. He wants Dr. Washington to come pay him a house call this afternoon."

"A house call? For what?"

"An adjustment."

"The judge needs an adjustment?"

"No. It's for Poochie."

"His wife?"

"Naw, that's his dog."

"But I thought he wasn't supposed to treat animals no more, doncha know."

Billy Joe closed his eyes and shook his head. "Deloris, you'll never learn."

"Learn what?"

"Whatever you need to. Now what is it you want with me?"

Deloris angled his head. "Let's go across the street and get us some coffee. I'll discuss everything with you over there. It's too crowded out here in the hallway to talk."

Billy Joe looked at his watch. "All right, let me see the doc a second, and I'll meet you over there. And by the way, the coffee will be on you."

***

Billy Joe took a seat opposite of Deloris. He leaned forward. "All right, what kinda problem you got now? You've always got problems. He looked at his watch. "And don't beat around the bush. Tell me straight out. I gotta be somewhere in about thirty minutes."

Before he could respond, a waitress, a black woman with silver hair, sidled up to their booth. "Y'all ain't want nothing but coffee, right?"

Billy Joe inclined his head toward the woman. "Deloris, did you know LaRue here, she could tell fortunes?" He slumped back in the booth. "There's the proof right there. She knew exactly what we wanted. How'd you know we wanted coffee, LaRue? Tell us. What's your secret? We won't tell nobody. Will we, Deloris?"

"I won't, but he will," Deloris said, pointing to Billy Joe. "He can't keep his mouth shut. But I have to tell you, I don't believe for one second you can tell somebody what's gonna happen in the future. If you could, you'd've brought our coffee when you come over here."

"You done found me out, Lawyer Meek. Yessir, you one clever man. Back directly."

Deloris waited until LaRue walked beyond earshot before he said anything to Billy Joe.

"This morning early—and I mean early—I got a long-distance telephone call from Ginger Childree."

"Yeah?"

"Yeah. She called to tell me they'd arrested her for stealing and for assault with intent to kill. The police claim she stole Kuddles back from Jimmy Holcomb and also took a shot at him. She said—"

Billy Joe raised his hand, signaling Deloris to stop. "Hold on a minute. Don't say no more."

"What? Why come?" Deloris said, befuddled.

Billy Joe looked around, edged closer to the table, and spoke in a hushed tone. "Deloris, you gotta keep this to yourself until I can speak with Dixie and Sergeant Unthank. I wanna be the one to tell them."

Sergeant Unthank, a retired serviceman, was Dixie's relative who worked from time to time with Billy Joe as his investigator.

"Tell them? Tell them what?" Deloris said as LaRue approached their table with two mugs of coffee.

Billy Joe waited until after LaRue had served them before continuing. He spoke in a low tone. "This is gonna come as a shock to you, Deloris. Ever since the governor appointed Lamar Robinette to be the attorney general—you know after Attorney General Sloan got himself killed in that car wreck—they tell me he was drunk as a coot. Anyway, Lamar's been after me to join his staff and be one of his assistants."

"What!?"

"I'm gonna quit private practice and become an assistant attorney general. Me and Lamar, we've gone back and forth about it. Bottom line, last night I finally agreed to do it. I figure this way I'll get me a whole lot of trial experience, which I'm not getting right now, things being the way they are. The experience I'll get working there will sure help me once I go back in private practice, maybe in a few years. I'll be trying a lot of condemnation cases for the highway department, he told me. You know, getting right-of-ways for controlled-access highways."

The news stunned Deloris. "I don't know what to say, Billy Joe."

Billy Joe's chin dropped to his chest. "I dreaded telling you." He sucked in air between his teeth. "And I really, really dread telling Dixie. Don't even like to think about it, if you wanna know the truth. I don't know how she's gonna react. You know how she can be. Least little thing will set her off. Ever seen her mad? Smoke pure comes outta both her nose and her ears."

Deloris laughed. "I've seen her mad, but I never saw no smoke—just the fire." He took a sip of his coffee. "Tell me this, can Dixie go with you and be your secretary?"

"I asked Lamar about letting me bring her, first thing."

"And?"

"He told me no, they already had a secretary in the office who'd be assigned to me. She's this old woman who's been with the office since the Pilgrims landed—where was it, Delaware?"

"I'm not sure. I remember the teacher telling us about this big rock they had there. Name's the same as a car. That's all I remember about it. I didn't do too good in history."

"What did you do good in?"

Deloris dropped his chin. "Nothing, I don't reckon."

"It's a Plymouth," Billy Joe announced.

"What is?"

"The rock those Pilgrims stepped on."

"Oh."

Billy Joe exhaled. "Well, anyway he tells me the woman even does a lot of their pleadings, even writes attorney general opinions, and stuff, and she'll be the one who's supposed to teach me everything about the office and so forth. She's the one who broke him in. Bottom line, I can't bring Dixie. My investigator neither." Billy Joe fell back in the booth. "Not being able to take them along with me is one reason it took me a while to tell Lamar I'd do it."

"Assistant Attorney General William Joseph Pratt," Deloris said, shaking his head. "I'll be durn. You'll be living there in the capital city with all those big-shot politicians, and you'll be bowing and scraping."

"Not me."

"Wanna bet?"

Deloris tasted his coffee and frowned. He poured more cream into his cup. "I don't know who I'm gonna be able to talk to now when I got me something I don't know what to do with, you being way up there and me way down here and you being busy going all over the state. I'm gonna be lost. You're the only lawyer friend I got, Billy Joe. You know I've always leaned on you. Ever since law school, I've done it." He took another sip of his coffee.

"I know, Deloris. I know. I'm sorry. Truly, I am."

Deloris mulled over Billy Joe's disclosure.

Billy Joe raised his coffee cup and set it back. "You know something? I just had me a brilliant thought."

"What?"

"Why don't you hire her, Deloris?"

"Hire who?"

"Dixie. Sergeant Unthank too."

Deloris' mouth fell open. "Are you serious? I'm barely able to support my ownself, Billy Joe. There ain't no way I could hire one person, much less two."

"But you wouldn't have to pay Unthank anything, doncha see. He's got his service pension, plus he married to a woman who's loaded with money. Anyway, I don't pay him a regular salary, but I will slip him a little something occasionally when I can afford it."

Deloris felt his chest tighten. "Even if I could afford to hire Dixie, I don't have me a real office to put her in. And I don't know if I want me one, either. See, right now, I don't have office rent to pay—you know. Heck, outside of oil and gas for my truck and the little bit I spend on its upkeep and a couple of other things, I don't have much in the way of business expenses."

Billy Joe raised his shoulders and let them drop. "Well, it was just a thought." He drank a bit of his coffee. "Lord, I sure dread telling Dixie."

"Well, you could tell her you did ask about them letting you bring her and Unthank along. That might could make it go a little easier for you."

"Yeah, I'd already planned to do that. But Dixie, she's not gonna believe me, if I know her, and I do." Billy Joe swallowed the last of his coffee, stood, and threw a quarter tip onto the table. "Gotta go and get this over with. See you later. I'll let you know what happens—provided, you know, Dixie doesn't kill me when I tell her what I'm about to do."

***

A knock on his driver-side door awoke Deloris from his mid-afternoon snooze. Rubbing his eyes, he made his way from the office area of his truck into the cab and peeped out the window. There stood Dixie St. John, her face drawn tight, her lips pressed together, her eyes aflame. Deloris opened the door as Dixie stepped back. He looked for the smoke Billy Joe had talked about.

"Well now, what's wrong?" he said, stepping to the ground.

"You know already. We need to talk, you and me. I'm so mad at Billy Joe I could kill him." She balled her fists. "Oh, that man, that horrible man!"

"He's told you about him closing down shop and jumping into the public trough, hasn't he?"

Dixie did not respond.

Deloris looked at his watch. "Uh-oh," he said."

"What?"

"Sorry. I gotta head upcountry. A client of mine is in jail up there and her bond hearing is this afternoon. Gotta go."

"I'll ride with you. I'm not going back there—not ever again."

"You mean to Billy Joe's?"

"Bingo."

Before Deloris could say anything, Dixie walked around the front of the truck and jerked open the passenger-side door. She plopped herself onto the passenger seat. "Back her out," she ordered.

Deloris turned and looked at her, his mouth agape. "You're not serious? You wanna ride with me all the way to Greenfield?"

"Yes."

"But I don't know what time I'll get back, Dixie. I gotta be in court, and I'll also need to confer with my client after we get done there. I just don't how long it's gonna take me to do everything. I know it'll probably be late."

"I don't care." She jerked a thumb over her shoulder. "Let's get a move on."

"Maybe this'll make you care. The client is Ginger Childree. She's been arrested for robbery and assault with a deadly weapon. The police claim she took a shot at Holcomb and stole Kuddles back from him."

"Ginger? No way. She may be a little off, if you know what I mean, but she's not a thief and she's not the type of person who'd hurt somebody. For one thing, she's not big enough to hurt a fly."

"I thought you didn't like her."

"I don't."

"So, why do you wanna go?"

"It's not about her. It's about me. I need—excuse my French—to get the hell outta Dodge, even if it means riding all the way to Greenfield with you and watching you get some whining little fruitcake out of the slammer." Dixie cocked her head and twirled her finger. "Now, can we please go, or have I gotta drive this stupid thing?"

CHAPTER SEVEN

When Deloris and Dixie arrived at the courthouse, they found the sheriff had already transported Ginger to the magistrate's courtroom. She sat with several other prisoners in the petit jury box, each of them handcuffed and shackled. Deloris had never seen Ginger looking so bad and forlorn, what with her hair disheveled, her face unpainted, and her clothes wrinkled. Ginger apparently had not seen Deloris and Dixie enter the courtroom. She kept her eyes fixed to the floor, as did the other prisoners who sat with heads bowed. The only sounds in the small, drab courtroom came from motor vehicle traffic outside.

Other than for the prisoners, two deputy sheriffs, a constable, a court clerk, and several lawyers whom Deloris did not know, the courtroom appeared otherwise empty.

As they stood there, Deloris whispered to Dixie, "I don't see Wally in here. Reckon he's coming?"

Dixie did not answer, if she heard him at all. Her attention seemed centered on finding a place to sit. After a moment, she took a seat on a front bench.

Deloris slipped inside the well of the courtroom and headed toward the court clerk, a heavy woman with heavy brown, heavy red lips, heavy makeup, heavy perfume, and heavy costume jewelry—the only things light about her were her skin and icy-blue eyes. The center of attraction, she sat in front of and below the magistrate's desk or bench, arranging papers and, without so much as a glance at them, rubber-stamping others with loud blows.

"Excuse me, ma'am," Deloris said.

The woman gave Deloris the once-over, fluttering her painted eyelids and crooking her head to the side. "Why yes, honey. Good morning. What can I do for you, precious?"

Deloris inclined his head toward the jury box. "My name is Deloris Meek, ma'am. I'm a lawyer. I'm here representing the pretty little lady over there in the jury box."

The clerk smiled. "I'm Miss Maxine Tumbleton, the deputy clerk assigned to Judge Metcalf's court. Who'd you say you're representing, honey?"

Deloris turned and pointed. "The lady over yonder."

"She got a name?"

"Oh, yes ma'am. Sorry. It's Ginger Childree."

Deloris glanced over at the jury box. For the first time, he noticed Ginger had recognized his presence. She had raised her head and smiled at him, but only for a couple of seconds.

Maxine shuffled through a stack of blue papers on her desk and withdrew two. "Sweetie, I've got two warrants here with her name on them. One's for robbery and the other's for assault." She opened the second warrant. "Hmmmmm. Says she shot at a preacher. My, my. That little ol' thing did all that? What is this world coming to? Assaults on preachers."

"Well, that's what they say."

"The judge, he'll be out here in a moment. More than likely, he'll let her sign a personal recognizance, provided she doesn't have a criminal record. So, if you don't mind, honey, please take your seat. I'll see to it we won't make you wait long."

Deloris nodded his okay. He waved to Ginger as he turned and sat down beside Dixie on one of the front-row benches.

The magistrate entered the courtroom without any fanfare at all and with no one ordering all present to stand; however, the lawyers stood, most likely out of habit. A tall, clean-shaven man, the magistrate wore no robe. He spoke a soft greeting to all present and folded himself into the high-back leather chair behind his desk.

"All right, Miss Tumbleton," he said as he leaned far back in his chair and crossed his long legs. "Let me have the first one, please ma'am."

Maxine pulled a warrant from a stack and gestured at a lawyer at one of the two counsel tables inside the rail. "Your Honor," she said, standing," this is a warrant served on the defendant Odis L. 'Pig' Galloway, Jr. It says he shoplifted some things from Greenfield Pharmacy downtown."

The magistrate bolted forward and took the warrant from Maxine. "All right, Pig. Come on around, please sir." He looked over the lawyers behind the counsel tables. "One you lawyers represent him?"

A handsome, young, redheaded, well-dressed attorney in a dark navy-blue suit and red tie stepped forward, holding a flat briefcase. "I do, Your Honor. By appointment."

The lawyer waited as Galloway, a man well into his twilight years, rose from his place in the jury box and shuffled toward the bench, wheezing all the way.

Dixie leaned in close to Deloris. "How come you can't dress like him? He's kinda cute."

"Which one you talking about?"

"The young lawyer, silly," she whispered.

"I thought you were talking about the old geezer," Deloris whispered back.

The magistrate read over the warrant as the defendant and his lawyer stood together, neither speaking to the other. "Pig," the magistrate said as he set the warrant aside, "if memory serves, this is maybe the fifth time I've had you in my courtroom for shoplifting or petty larceny. Am I right?"

Before Galloway could answer, his lawyer Rayford Deal spoke for him. "Yes, sir. But three of the warrants got dismissed, Your Honor."

"But what about the fourth one, the one they didn't dismiss, Mr. Deal?"

"It's not been tried yet, Your Honor, although it was set for trial one time."

"Not tried? What's the date of the offense?"

"It was supposed to've been tried three years ago last Thursday, Your Honor, but the court never called it for trial. However, Mr. Galloway and I, we were both in court at the scheduled time ready for trial. We sat there all day, as a matter of fact. The sign-in sheet should show our attendance."

"Say it would? Three years ago, you say? My goodness gracious. Whoever the magistrate was, the governor ought to remove him from office, if you ask me. And do it forthwith. Know which magistrate it got assigned to?"

Deal hung his head and murmured his response as the magistrate, a hand cupped to his ear, leaned toward counsel.

"I didn't hear you, Mr. Deal."

"Sorry, Your Honor, sir. "I said it was you, sir."

The magistrate's face flushed. "Well, we've kinda gotten a little behind. We ain't never had the help we needed, have we Miss Tumbleton?

"No, sir," his clerk answered in a strained voice. She closed her eyes and took a deep breath.

"Bond for this offense—the fifth one—I'll set at one hundred dollars. He can sign a personal recognizance. I'll put the old one down for us to try it sometime next month. Remind me, Miss Tumbleton, to schedule Pig's old case for trial. First, though, we might better contact the store he stole from and see if they're still interested in prosecuting him. Call them when we get done here this morning. By the way, Mr. Deal, before you and Pig leave us, the bond for the one we didn't dispose of, it continues, understand? I think I'll let it stand for the new charges too. Okay?"

"Yes, sir, Judge. No problem," Deal replied.

"Okay, call the next one, please ma'am."

"Judge," Maxine said, "if my memory serves, the store—Greenfield Pharmacy—it's changed hands since he was arrested."

"Still call them," the judge said.

Maxine wrote something on a yellow pad. "Yes, sir."

With warrants in hand, Maxine stood and smiled at Deloris. "Your Honor, this next case involves two warrants against Miss Ginger Childree. She's represented by Deloris Meek, Esquire." She motioned to Deloris. "You can come forward." She turned toward the jury box and nodded at Ginger. "You too, honey. Come on up here now."

Ginger brushed back her matted hair as she stepped from the jury box to join Deloris at the bench. Meanwhile, the magistrate studied the warrants Maxine had handed him.

Judge Metcalf laid the warrants aside, stared at Deloris and Ginger, and stretched his neck as he appeared to search the courtroom. He settled back in his chair. "Miss Tumbleton, where's the lady lawyer?"

Maxine stood. "Sir?"

"The lady lawyer. Where's she? She come?"

"The lady lawyer?"

"She's apparently one of Miss Childree's lawyers?"

"Why, Your Honor, her lawyer's standing right next to her. She only has one."

"I thought you said she's represented by a woman named Deloris something or other?"

Deloris laughed. "No, sir. I'm a man, Your Honor."

"I can see that, but what you doing with a girl's name."

"No, sir, it's a boy's name, sir. I spell it with an 'i,' not with no 'e.' I get this all the time."

The magistrate raised his eyebrows. "Well, if you say so, okay. But it sure sounds like a girl's name to me." He cleared his throat. "I mean you no offense, sir. My apologies. In any case, tell me about your client, sir."

Deloris patted Ginger on the shoulder. "Your Honor, there's been a big mistake here. You see, Miss Childree—"

Judge Metcalf raised his hand, interrupting Deloris. "We're not here this morning to try the case, Mr. Meek. Just deal with bail, please sir. Nothing else. Tell me a little something about her, please sir."

Deloris nodded. "Yes, sir. Right. Miss Childree, she works for a local bottling plant. She inspects bottles for them. She's working there only for a little while, you know, to kinda tide her over until she gets her a new dummy."

" 'Gets her a new dummy?' You mean a new husband? Boyfriend?" The magistrate appeared confused.

"Oh, no, no, no, Judge. She's an actress. Well, sorta one. She's a ventriloquist. I guess they're actors or actresses. She's got her a TV show all lined up which is gonna be starting real soon on one of the local stations here in Greenfield. Before she can do it, though, she gotta have her a new dummy made to use on the show." He glanced at Ginger and looked back at the magistrate. "I'm assuming the TV station will still stand by their agreement. But I don't know if they will or not, what with this arrest and all—you know, the publicity. It may have killed any chance she had of doing the show."

Ginger dropped her chin to her chest and wiped her eyes as her lips quivered.

The judge picked up a warrant and appeared to read it. "What's this mean, Mr. Meek? The warrant alleges she stole Kuddles. Is that a dog? A cat? What?"

"It's a dummy, Your Honor. You know, like Charlie McCarthy is. Mortimer Snerd. Kuddles is her old one."

"Oh, I get it. Okay. What about the other warrant? It says she shot at an evangelist—a fella the warrant identifies as Brother Jimmy Holcomb. I've seen his tent there in Awenasa. Ridden by it a few times. Big thing."

Deloris eyed Ginger. "She denies doing what the warrant alleges, Your Honor."

"She got any prior record of having stolen anything or committed an assault? Any criminal record at all?"

Ginger shook her head.

"Matter of fact, Your Honor, up until recently, she's been doing the Lord's work as an evangelist," Deloris said.

The magistrate nodded. "I see." He gestured toward the two deputy sheriffs. "Either y'all know anything about these cases? I haven't been given anything other than the arrest warrants, which I reckon is par for the course."

Both men looked at each other with blank expressions.

Judge Metcalf gazed up at the ceiling a few seconds. "Okay, Mr. Meek. Bail is set at one hundred dollars on the robbery warrant and five hundred on the assault. She can sign a personal recognizance warrant. They got some forms downstairs you can use, Mr. Meek. Sign one for each offense and file them with the clerk of court. Sorry about the name business." He paused. "Next case, Miss Tumbleton."

Maxine stood and turned around. "Before we do it, Judge, could you give me a moment, please sir?"

Without waiting for the magistrate's response, Maxine caught Ginger and Deloris before they could exit the well of the courtroom. "Mr. Meek, honey," she said, tapping Deloris on his shoulder, "could you meet me about one-fifteen at Swing's across the street? I may can help you some."

***

Troubles and Kuddles

Patrons of Swing's Tavern, noted for its good food and its wall collection of golf clubs and framed, autographed pictures of famed golfers, either sat in a booth or at a counter for service. A pleasant odor of fresh-baked bread greeted customers the instant they came inside.

Precisely at one-fifteen p.m., Deloris, Dixie, and Ginger chose a booth, one near the front and far away from the Wurlitzer jukebox at the rear of the room. "Chapel of Love" by the Dixie Cups followed Al Hirt's "Java" onto the turntable before the jukebox fell silent, much to Deloris' relief. His enjoyment of the absence of music proved short lived. Less than a minute after Hirt blew his last note, a coin dropped into a wall box started spinning Manfred Mann's "Do Wah Diddy Diddy."

A shadow fell upon the table. "If you'll scoot your tight little hinny over, baby doll, I'll sit my big one down by you," Maxine Tumbleton said to Ginger. "I believe there's room."

Ginger slid over and hugged the wall as Maxine loaded her huge frame onto the seat, causing it to dip, squeak, and groan. "Have y'all ordered yet, honey?"

"No," Deloris said, "not yet. Whatcha recommend? What's good here?"

"Everything. I usually order the blue-plate special. Their steak sandwiches are the best in the world. Their Dixiecrats, they're real good too. Well, they're good if you like them."

"Couldn't you say that just about everything there is?" Dixie said.

"Dixiecrats? What are they?" Deloris asked.

Maxine sat straight in the booth with her shoulders back. "Nothing but a mustard-covered Polish sausage served on a slice of their good bread."

"That's it?" Deloris said.

"That's it, honey. Ol' Jeff Davis would've loved them. And you would too. But if you plan to order one, better get two, maybe three to fill you up." She patted her stomach.

Ginger smiled at Maxine. "Miss Tumbleton, I'll have to say the people in the clerk's office were very nice to us when we went by there a while ago for me to sign those bond forms."

"Well, good. I'll tell Mr. Jewell you said so. He's the clerk of court. He'll be glad to hear it." She smiled at Deloris. "I'm so glad y'all agreed to meet me here, sweetie."

Deloris studied Maxine for a moment. "Really? Well, what'd you mean when you said you could help us?"

Before she could answer, a woman in a green and white waitress uniform bumped against the table as she leaned in to distribute four menus and glasses of water. The woman stepped backwards. "Special today is oven-baked country-fried steak, mash potatoes and gravy, and English peas. Ice tea and yeast rolls come with it. Back in a second to get your order."

Maxine pitched forward and looked around. She spoke almost in a whisper. "I used to have a thing going with Jimbo, want you to know."

"Jimbo?" Deloris said.

Maxine giggled and fell back in the booth. "My pet name for Brother Holcomb."

Ginger, her eyes widen, turned and looked at her seatmate. "Say what now?"

Maxine patted Ginger's arm. "Oh, I went out with him some, Honey. Well, it wasn't so much of me going out with him as it was me staying in with him, if you catch my drift." She tee-heed. "I called what him and me done 'Airstreaming.' You know, he had him one of these Airstream trailers out behind his tabernacle."

Deloris blinked. "Tabernacle?"

"You know, his tent," Maxine said. "Jimbo called it a tabernacle. He claimed a tent was the only kind of real church you could have. He pointed out Paul made his living as a tentmaker, not as a bricklayer or carpenter."

"Are you telling us you slept with him in his Airstream?" Ginger asked, her eyes still on Maxine.

Maxine laughed. "That and other things, missy, and I'm not talking about fixing him peanut butter and jelly sandwiches neither."

"But didn't you know he's married?" Ginger said.

"Not at first, I didn't. I didn't see any wife around, and he didn't say nothing about having him one." Maxine took a sip of water and exhaled. "Ignorance is bliss, they say. I for one certainly found it to be that way with him." She became dreamy-eyed. "Blissful—blissful as a spring morning spent on a Pawley's Island hammock." She shivered. "Ooooo. Just thinking about it makes me. . . oh, never mind."

"What's your relationship with Brother Holcomb got to do with Ginger here, Miss Tumbleton?" Deloris said. "How can you help her?"

"Call me 'Maxine,' darling." She studied Deloris for a second or two. "You're kinda cute, you know that? Not real cute, but kinda cute. You could put your shoes under my bed anytime. But I'd want you to lose a little weight first." She slapped her hips and laughed. "Now ain't I'm one to talk, huh? Let me ask you something. You married, baby?"

Deloris' face warmed. "No, I'm not." He glanced around at Dixie.

Maxine's face broke into a huge smile. "Oh, that's great. We'll have to talk later, won't we? Never mind about what I said about you losing weight. Sometimes, I like 'em kinda big like you are. Know what my mama told me one time? She said, marry you a big man. He'll keep you warm in the winter and shade in the summer."

Maxine laughed at her own joke. No one else did.

Deloris pulled at his collar. His chest felt tight. "Miss Tumbleton, right now all I'm interested in, ma'am, is how you might can help Ginger here." Deloris' face and now his neck and ears burned.

Maxine moaned as she covered her top lip with her bottom one. "You sure know how to hurt a girl, doncha, big fella? Even so, I'll tell you about me and him. I'll do it because I wanna help little sister, here." She sighed. "I first met Brother Holcomb the night I thought I'd been saved."

"Yeah?" Deloris said, his head leaning to the side.

Maxine nodded. "Uh-huh. That night, his tent was filled to the gills, and the music, it was something else again. Real lively, upbeat. Why it looked like almost everybody there was singing and dancing and clapping and praising the Lord."

Heck, a whole bunch of the folks, why they pure got out in the aisles and commenced to dancing and carrying on. Some of them even went up front to do it. And the little kids, you should've seen them. They were so cute boogying around, precious little things. The organist, she kept playing 'Jesus on the Mainline' over and over again."

"Excuse me, ma'am," Deloris said, "when are you gonna tell us something that'll help Ginger here."

Maxine extended her leg beneath the table and rubbed her foot against Deloris' calf. "Hold your horses, sweetheart. You're kinda impatient, aren't you? I hope you don't like hurrying up in everything you do, baby?"

Deloris drew back his leg and looked at Dixie, concern written on his face. He feared she might have noticed what Maxine had done.

"Like I was telling you," Maxine said, "we were all singing and dancing to 'Jesus on the Mainline' and so forth. It's a kinda song that'll set your feet to dancing. I bet they must've played it for a good ten minutes or more. Seems like they couldn't let go of it—not that anybody wanted them to. "Heck, some folks got so in the spirit, would you believe they jumped up there on the platform where Jimbo and Brother Shiflet were and started dancing with them? They sure did.

"Every now and then, Jimbo'd reached down and pull somebody up there with him, and they hoofed it out, the two of them. Why, one old man who was using a walker, he came hopping to the front. He kept knocking folks out the way. And would you believe what Jimbo went and done? Why, he reached down for him and grabbed the old fella by one of his hands and, bless Jesus, he—the old man—he threw his walker down on the ground and him and Jimbo, the two of them, they just danced and danced. Well, they sorta danced, with Jimbo up there on the platform, leaning down, and the old man, him down below, panting and everything, trying to keep up.

"And you know what happened? The old man, he suddenly dropped down on the ground in a heap. Yeah, he sure did, right there in front of Jimbo. After a while, when he didn't get back up,

Jimbo motioned to a couple of ushers to come fetch him. They ran down to the front and hauled the old man off through the back of the tent."

Dixie muttered something to herself and directed cold, dead eyes at Maxine. "You know, I wish you'd get to the point."

Maxine ignored Dixie's remark. "Guess what I went and done right after that? Me, crazy me, I found myself up there with Jimbo somehow, and me and him, we danced like we were out on a hot date at some low-down honky-tonk on the outskirts of town. He had me twirling all around and around. I was ducking under Jimbo's arm, shaking my big ol' fanny, doing steps, putting one foot out in front of the other, twisting, and all. I tell you what's a fact, it just about done me in." She fanned herself with her hand.

Before Maxine could resume, the waitress appeared with an order pad. "Y'all ready?" She pulled a pencil from the bob of hair atop her head.

Once the waitress left to turn in the four orders, Maxine went on with her report. "Anyway, later on, when Jimbo'd got done with his preaching, he gave an invitation for anybody whose heart'd been warmed to come forward.

"Right then, it wasn't only my heart which had gotten warm." Maxine fanned herself a couple of times with her hand. "Heck, I was hot all over, I'll tell you that. So, I traipsed down front and knelt while Jimbo prayed over me and all those others who'd answered the altar call.

"After he got done praying, he took me by the hand and helped me get to my feet. While he was doing it, he squeezed my hand real tight. Then he kissed me on my cheek and whispered to me. He said, 'Bless you, sister, and listen to what I'm about to tell you. After the service, I want you to go to my trailer out back. It's the Airstream. I'll meet you there.'

"I winked him an okay, and he let go my hand, smiling that pretty smile of his. I tell y'all one thing. It was sorta like the title to that old-time revival hymn, 'Love Lifted Me.' I felt lifted by love. I sure did. Between you and me, that wasn't all love lifted that evening or pulled down either. No, sir."

Dixie looked at Ginger, and Ginger looked at Dixie. Both women sat drop-mouthed and wide-eyed. Ginger also had her hand to her throat. Deloris sat with his arms crossed, his head to the side, and his tongue against his upper lip.

"A little while later, when the service got done with, I hung around until the tent pretty much emptied out and all those folks with the crusade had gone. I then moseyed on around to the back of the tent and waited for him by this silver-looking trailer."

Maxine smiled in a coy kind of way. "When he finally left his tabernacle and came back to where I was at—he had to wait to see how the offering went, he told me, otherwise he'd been right on out—he said he was plumb beat down from all the preaching and singing he had to do and said what he needed was to get him something to drink and some love, mercy, and grace and a whole lot of the first one—you know, love." She laughed. "He kinda winked when he told me that. He asked me if I wanted something to wet my whistle too, and I told him yeah, I could use me a little something."

Maxine bumped herself back against the wall. "So, me and him, we stepped inside his trailer, and I went and sat on his couch and kinda looked around, you know, while he went to the fridge there in the kitchen part. I was kinda surprised to see sitting over in the corner this big, cute doll. But seeing it wasn't the only surprise I got. He opened his refrigerator and got us out two beers."

"He handed me my beer and sat himself down next to me and propped his feet on the coffee table and put his arm around me and started stroking my arm, tickling it like, with his fingers." Maxine wrapped her arms around her body. "Oh, it makes me tingle all inside when I think about it. Ooooeee."

"The doll, as you call it, that was my ventriloquist dummy, Kuddles," Ginger said, almost as an afterthought.

Maxine nodded. "Yeah, that's what he told me when I asked him about it later on, only he said it was his, but he didn't know how to use it real good—you know, throw his voice. I asked him how come he had it if he couldn't use it, and he said he'd practiced doing it but hadn't been able to get the hang of it yet. He never said anything about you. But he did call the dummy 'Kuddles,' which I thought was kinda cute."

"So, the two of y'all drank a beer together?" Deloris asked, egging her on.

"Not 'a beer,' honey. Several beers."

"You never questioned him about why a preacher'd be drinking beer?" Deloris asked.

"Sure, I did. Know what he said? He said, 'Show me in the Bible where Jesus said it was a sin to drink beer.' Well, of course, I couldn't do that."

"How long did you stay there?" Deloris asked.

"That first night?" Maxine blushed. "Most of the night. I'd liked to have stayed the whole night, but I had to get up the next morning and be at work at the magistrate's."

"And you're telling us you didn't know he was married?" Ginger asked, her disgust with Maxine evident in her tone.

"Not then, I didn't. Later on, though, I asked him whether he'd ever been married. He told me he had been, but his wife had done run off with a man ten years younger than she was, a fella who worked as one of his tent men—you know, somebody who took care of the tent, helped put it up and all."

The waitress appeared with the four orders and served them.

As the waitress departed the booth, Deloris tasted the ice tea. "So, he told you his wife had run off with another man, did he?"

"Right, uh-huh," Maxine said. "That turned out to be a big ol lie, I come to find out. Why, his wife, she hadn't run off at all. She'd gone back home to take care of her poor ol' sick mama way, way out yonder in Nebraska."

"How'd you learn that? He tell you?"

"Oh no. His wife turned up one day outta the clear blue. She caught me and him together there in the trailer one Sunday afternoon, both us naked as a pair of jaybirds. She walked right in on us, big as you please."

"I bet that scared the dickens outta you," Deloris said, laughing. He looked around at Dixie and over at Ginger to gage their reaction. Neither of them laughed or seemed amused in the slightest.

"Scared me? Who? Her? Not that scrawny thing? She wasn't nothing but skin and bones. Looked like a haint. She couldn't hurt a fly. Had she tried anything, I could've broken her in half—like she was a crab leg—no, a toothpick."

"What'd she do when she caught y'all?" Deloris asked.

"Nothing but hand me my bloomers and my bra and my slip and said it was high time for me to have a little talk with Jesus. She watched me put my clothes back on, telling me while I did it I wasn't the first woman she'd caught him with and she expected I wouldn't be the last one neither."

"How did the reverend react at y'all being caught?" Dixie asked.

"He laughed about it. So, instead of me being mad or angry or embarrassed with her catching me and him together, I started feeling right sorry for her and even a little guilty. I sure did, especially after she told me what she'd been doing."

Maxine took a bite of her steak, chewed it for few seconds, and washed it down with her tea.

"Soon as I got my hair combed and put me on a little lipstick, I headed for the door. But before I left, I turned and asked him how could a man of God carry on like he did, lying to me about his wife and sleeping around with me and God knows how many other women? Know what he said? He said everything'd be all right. If King David could do it and be forgiven, so could he.

"And when he told me this, he grabbed hold of his wife and hugged her real tight, saying to her 'Ain't that right, sweetheart.' And you know what she did? She smiled back at him and said, 'Right as rain. Praise the Lord. If He can forgive you, darling Jim, I can too.' Next thing you know, she'd kissed him right smack on his lips and rubbed up against him. She was like a dog in heat, throwing a leg around one of his as they stood there."

Deloris nodded at Ginger. "Okay now. Why are you telling us all this? You don't know Ginger here. You don't know me."

"Why? Because, sweetheart, I wanna see him get what's coming to him. He made a fool outta me, that's why—not telling me the truth about his wife and all, taking advantage of me. I really thought he cared something for me, but he didn't. He just wanted to use me, that's all. After I left him and his wife in the Airstream that Sunday and the more I thought about everything, the madder I got." She tapped the table. "And I'm still mad about it."

"Yeah, well how can what you've told us help my client?" Deloris asked.

"Honey, have I got to draw you a picture and get me out some crayons and color it for you? It's what they called believability or credibility. Won't nobody ever believe the so-called Reverend Dr. Jimmy Holcomb when I get through telling everything I know about the sorry thing and how he did me—how he used me, lied to me and everything. If he's a man of God, it's got to be one of them small "g" ones. Doctor—doctor my fanny. What I didn't realize when I answered Brother Holcomb's altar call that night was I wasn't giving my heart and soul over to Jesus Christ. Oh no, I was giving my heart and body over to Brother Jimmy Holcomb. I'll tell y'all one thing. He's played hell taking them like he did."

Dixie scoffed. "How can you say with a straight face you didn't realize what you were doing? Give me a break. You sure as heck did. You knew exactly what you were doing when you went into that trailer with him." She elbowed Deloris and dipped her head toward Maxine. "I'm telling you one thing, Deloris Meek, little Miss Ginger'll be in prison before the sun goes down if you use this woman as a defense witness. There's no telling what she'd do or say, believe me. I wouldn't trust her as far as I could throw her. And that'd be no farther than a quarter inch."

"Hey, young lady, I dare you," Maxine said, raising her voice and aiming a hard stare at Dixie, "I don't appreciate at all what you're implying. You don't even know me."

Dixie stared back equally as hard. "No, I don't. But I know your type. And as for your not appreciating what you said I, as you phrased it, 'implied' about you just now, guess what. I don't care. And another thing, I didn't imply it. I said it straight out."

"You two. Y'all hold it down," Deloris said, looking around the room and embarrassed by their behavior. "People are looking at us."

Wondering if he should apologize for Dixie's conduct, Deloris looked at Maxine. What he saw unsettled him.

She sat for a moment with squinted eyes, retracted shoulders, and trembling lips. Her large breasts rose and fell as she took deep breaths. After a moment and with her head held low, she smiled and patted her lips with a napkin. "If y'all will excuse me," she said in a soft, calm voice as she slid out of the booth.

As she walked away, Maxine said loud enough for Deloris and his table companions to hear, "Try to help somebody and this . . . Well, if they don't want my help . . ."

CHAPTER EIGHT

"Mr. Meek," Deloris heard a deep, accented voice call out as he exited the Harvester's State Bank and Trust Company. He turned to see walking toward him a figure from his recent past, Jade Ziglar.

Ziglar quicken his pace. "Glad I caught you. I was headed your way."

Deloris stopped and waited for Ziglar to come abreast with him. "Morning," he said, extending a hand toward the squat but powerfully built man.

Ziglar gripped Deloris' hand so tightly he thought his hand would not survive the greeting intact.

Deloris wrenched his hand free and rubbed his sore fingers. "I'm surprised to see you, Mr. Ziglar."

"Yeah?"

"Well, yeah. You say you were coming to see me?"

"Some place we can talk?"

Deloris nodded. "There's Grubb's about a block away. That's a café. Or, we can go to my office. It's a little bit farther to walk."

"Best we go to your office."

When the two men reached his truck, Deloris removed two lawn chairs from the back and set them in a shaded spot outside. "Okay if we sit out here? It's pretty nice out this morning."

Their presence disturbed several crows nearby. The black, winged creatures cawed and hopped around, almost defiantly but they eventually flew away.

Ziglar selected a chair without comment and lit a cigar as he sat.

Deloris stood behind the empty chair. "Those crows you saw just now—"

"Yeah? What about them?"

Deloris pointed to his truck. "Odd thing. I kept finding my windshield wipers tore up. Come to find out, it was the crows done it."

"Crows?"

Deloris took a seat. "Yeah. Way I got them to stop was I tied me a couple of red balloons to the wipers. A veterinarian told me to try that and see what would happen." Deloris crossed his legs. "All right, sir, tell me what's on your mind?"

Ziglar blew a smoke ring, but a slight breeze dissipated the ring before it travelled half a foot. "I found my man."

Deloris acted nonchalant, maintaining a blank face. "Who? Wally Teal? I'm not surprised."

"His real name is Fromberg. Eli Fromberg."

"I knew that."

"He's working in a hospital.

"Right. In Greenfield. As an orderly."

"You knew that too?

"Just found out about it. So now what?"

"That's what I wanna talk to you about. I'll pay you to listen."

Ziglar had spoken the magic words, "pay you."

"I'm all ears," Deloris said, glancing at his watch. "Clock's ticking."

"As you know, we've been looking for Fromberg for some time now."

"Yeah, but I don't know how come."

Ziglar grunted. "Okay, I'm authorized to tell you. Sometime ago Fromberg's uncle Izzy Goldmann—his mother's brother—was found dead in his townhouse after he didn't come to his office for several days running. He'd been shot. Funny thing, there was no sign of a break-in or any sign of a struggle. Far as could be determined, nothing appeared missing."

"Suicide perhaps?"

"No. He was shot in the back of the head, execution style."

"So, how does Wally, that is, Fromberg figure in?"

"From what the police tell me, he was the last person to see Goldmann alive. They were seen having dinner together at a restaurant earlier that evening. After that, Fromberg, he kinda vanished like."

"So, I gather the police suspect him of killing Goldmann?"

"Right, but they lack the evidence to tie him to it. Right now, they don't have any. No direct evidence, they don't."

"Circumstantial evidence?"

"Only this. As far as the police can determine, Fromberg is the only person who would've benefitted by Goldmann's death. Plus, Fromberg was seen with Goldmann the night they figured he got killed and Fromberg disappeared soon after. I'm sure you've heard the saying, 'the wicked fleeth when no man pursueth,' right? From the Bible."

Deloris nodded. "And how's Fromberg's supposed to have benefitted?"

"How? He stands to inherit everything Goldmann owned, that's how. His holdings are worth millions of dollars. And Fromberg? He doesn't have the proverbial pot."

Deloris scratched the back of his head. "Millions of dollars, huh?" He paused. "Exactly where do you fit in, Mr. Ziglar, in all this?"

"The executor of the estate, a bank in New Jersey, hired me to help locate Fromberg."

"Well, you did that—found him, I mean. Have you spoken to him yet?"

Ziglar shook his head. "Not yet."

"Why not?"

Ziglar took a drag on his cigar and allowed the smoke to escape through his mouth and nose simultaneously. "Since he's a suspect in a murder investigation, we don't want him to know we are aware of his whereabouts—not until we are certain about whether he had a hand in his uncle's murder, we don't. You see, Mr. Goldmann's will provided Fromberg's interest wouldn't vest until the time of distribution of his property. Way it's been explained to me, under the law, if Fromberg bears any responsibility for the murder of Mr. Goldmann, Fromberg—"

"I know, he couldn't inherit anything, and the estate would pass to somebody else under the terms of the will, and if the will doesn't name anybody else or doesn't have a residuary clause, it'd become an intestate estate. I remember that much from law school." Deloris felt pleased with himself for remembering that principle of the law.

"In which case—"

"It'd go to the next of kin," Deloris said, interrupting. "With the uncle being as rich as I gather he must've been to warrant all this attention, God knows how many folks out there may fit that definition. I expect there'll be a passel."

"A what, Mr. Meek?"

"Never mind." Deloris stared at Ziglar for a moment. "Whatcha want from me, Mr. Ziglar. Why come you're telling me all this, sir."

Ziglar eyed Deloris, appearing to study him. "Tell you what. I like a fella who likes to get right to the point. Okay, this is the reason I wanted to talk to you some more. After I told my client about our prior conversation, it was suggested I try to talk you into helping us keep an eye on Fromberg and your ears open— you know, keeping us informed about his whereabouts and about anything he might say that's help us or the police with the murder investigation. You can do it pretty much through his former partner, the Childree woman. You've got a connection with her, being you represented her recently. And you and he, you share a history."

"I'll say." Deloris thought of the incident in Louisiana.

"Of course, we'd pay you well for your services. In fact, we'd pay you extremely well."

Deloris mulled over Ziglar's offer. "Basically, you want me to spy on Wally without him, or anybody else for that matter, knowing I'm doing it. That's pretty much it, isn't it?"

Ziglar hunched his shoulders and drew in more tobacco smoke and exhaled it. "I suppose. Well, yeah, that's right. You could say that."

"I dunno, Mr. Ziglar. I'm a lawyer. Not no spy." Deloris paused a moment. "But I'll tell you what, I know an excellent private detective who's about to be unemployed." Deloris' thought was of Bible Unthank, Billy Joe Pratt's investigator.

"Does he know Fromberg? Ever had any close contact with him?"

"Not's I know of."

Ziglar shook his head. "See, that'd be a problem. We want somebody who's been close to him before. Somebody he might trust. See what I mean? He trusts you. He trusts the Childree girl."

"What you're saying is you want somebody that'd be willing to betray a trust, don't you?"

"Naw. Not anything like that."

Deloris smiled and ran a hand through his hair. "I'm sorry, Mr. Ziglar. I'm not your man. I don't believe there ever was a time in my life when I betrayed somebody's trust. I'm not about to do that now. I know I'm not the smartest lawyer around, but I like for folks to believe they can trust me." Deloris stood. "Thank you, sir. I've got some work I gotta do today. Good morning, sir."

"But Mr. Meek, consider the money we can pay you," Ziglar said, still seated. "Right now, I'm authorized to pay you—"

Without saying another word, Deloris folded his lawn chair, slid it inside his truck, and ambled around to the driver side. He opened the door, pausing long enough to address Ziglar. "When you get ready to leave, would you do me a favor? Please set my lawn chair against the wall there, if you don't mind. It should be all right. Oh yeah, and go next door to Kingry's Insurance and give the secretary out front fifteen dollars and tell her it's for me. My time, doncha know."

Deloris slipped in behind the steering wheel, started the motor, and backed out of the parking space. As he drove away, he watched in the outside rearview mirror as Ziglar, a folded lawn chair in his hands, shook his head, a cigar still in his mouth.

***

Deloris pulled into his parking spot about an hour later. Relieved at seeing his lawn chair resting against the wall of Kingry Insurance and Jade Ziglar nowhere in sight, he cut the motor and exited his truck. Rather than attend to matters on his desk deserving of his attention, his life-long affliction of procrastination took hold and directed him next door to check whether he had received any telephone calls and whether Ziglar had indeed left him any money.

When he entered Kingry's, the presence of Dixie St. John took him by surprise. She sat with her back to the front door, talking to the secretary who handled his calls and helped him with whatever typing he needed.

"Whatcha you doing here, Dixie?" he asked.

She turned around and peered at him. "Waiting on you to come to work."

"I've been at work."

Dixie, a tongue to her cheek, closed her eyes and nodded. "Uh-huh. Of course, you have."

"Well, I have." Deloris looked upon Miss Opal Tice being as much of an office fixture at Kingry Insurance as its wooden file cabinets and hardwood floors. "Miss Tice, did a fella come by here and leave me an envelope this morning?"

"An envelope?" Opal replied. "Uh, no."

Deloris frowned and cursed to himself. He really had not expected Ziglar to pay him for the time Ziglar spent with him earlier that day.

Opal smiled. "But he did leave you a couple of pictures?"

Deloris gritted his teeth. He thought he saw Opal wink at Dixie. "Pictures? What kinda pictures?"

"Two fellas. Alexander Hamilton and Abe Lincoln," Opal said with a laugh as she handed Deloris fifteen dollars.

Dixie also laughed.

"You had me going there, Miss Tice." Deloris pocketed the money, feeling a small measure of guilt over his jumping to the wrong conclusion about Ziglar.

He smiled at Miss Tice's visitor. "So, what'd you want with me, Dixie?"

Dixie stood. "Nice seeing you, Miss Tice." She angled her head toward Deloris. "Gotta talk to this guy. Enjoyed seeing you. Call me, and we'll go to lunch sometime."

As Deloris and Dixie walked toward his truck, he inquired about what she wanted.

"Billy Joe sent me. We've come up with a deal for you."

"We?"

"Yeah. Me and him. Mostly me."

Deloris opened a rear door to his truck. "What kinda deal? And why come he didn't come his ownself to tell me about it?"

Troubles and Kuddles

Dixie grabbed the chair Ziglar had left propped against the wall and unfolded it. "Let's sit outside."

"Suits me," Deloris said. He withdrew the other chair from inside the truck and set it up. "Okay. Shoot."

Dixie sat and straightened her skirt. Deloris also sat.

"Here's the deal. Late yesterday afternoon, the attorney general called Billy Joe and said he wanted him to come immediately. Billy Joe told him he just couldn't drop everything and do that because he had some things in the fire. The attorney general would have none of it and told Billy Joe he'd have to start next week if he wanted to be his assistant, and if he couldn't do that, he'd take his offer off the board and he'd get somebody else. Well, anyway, Billy Joe promised to let him know something in a day or two.

"After he got off the phone and told me what the attorney general had said, I asked him what he was gonna do, and he said he didn't know of anything at the moment and wanted to know if I had any ideas. You know me. I'm never without any ideas."

Deloris thought, *That's the damn truth.*

"Bottom line, this is what we decided on, me and him. And I don't wanna hear any bellyaching from you about it. Got that?"

Deloris drew back. "What are you talking about?"

Dixie bent forward. "This is what we've decided to do."

"You and Billy Joe?"

Dixie made a face. "Who else have I been talking about?" Dixie shook her head and closed her eyes while taking a quick breath. "What we're gonna do is this. You will move into his law office and take over all his cases, splitting any fees you get from handling them fifty-fifty. I'll work as your secretary and help you with them. I know more about them than Billy Joe does anyway. Sergeant Unthank, he'll stay on as well. He's agreed to do it." Dixie pointed to the truck. "Of course, this'll mean you'll have to do away with that stupid thing."

"The hell you say."

"We can talk about it later."

Deloris could hardly believe his ears. "So, you and Billy Joe, y'all've decided I'll take over his law practice, have you?"

Dixie crossed her arms. A big smile spread across her face. "Yep, we sure have. And don't forget Sergeant Unthank. He was in on it too." She stared at Deloris. "What? You got a problem with it?"

Deloris' mouth dropped open. "You kidding me? First off, I can't afford to pay office rent. That's why come I got me a truck, or didn't you know that? Some months, I can't hardly afford to buy the gas to even run the durn thing, doncha know. And there's this. I sure as heck can't afford to pay you. The first thing I'd have to do is to let you go. I'm not quite ready for bankruptcy yet, you see. So, yeah I've got a problem with it. A real big one."

Dixie uncrossed her arm and smiled. "Deloris, Deloris, Deloris. How long have you known me? Don't you know I can do anything? Who does the title searches at Billy Joe's office? Me, that's who. Billy Joe couldn't check a land title if his life depended on it. I bet you couldn't either. Heck, both of you even have trouble with street addresses. Wouldn't you think I'd have everything, and I mean everything, all worked out before I would even mention any of this to you? Give me some credit, why don't you? Sometimes—"

"What do you mean 'worked out'?"

"I mean 'worked out' as in 'I've got the answers to all the problems involved' in the move. Let's see, for the office rent and utilities, Billy Joe has already paid three-months' rent in advance. It's not much as rental space goes, but it suffices. He pays the rent quarterly. He's willing to pay half of the future rents and utilities for an additional three quarters. You can pay them out of his portions of the fees you'll be getting from handling the files he's gonna leave you with. Now that sounds perfectly fair to me. And allow me to let you in on a little secret, the title work other lawyers and First Federal and some of the other loaning institutions refer to us, they'll usually take care of the overhead, most of it anyway— least that's the way it's been here lately with me and Billy Joe.

"And if you're worried about Sergeant Unthank, he doesn't get a salary. He comes and helps out mainly to get away from his old lady who's got, by the way, more money than Carter's got liver pills, or so he tells me. Plus, he's got his Army retirement to fall back on and all that—you know, medical care and the VA to boot. Sometimes, Billy Joe, he'd slip him some money whenever Unthank helped him with a case. He's worth every dime Billy Joe ever paid him, believe me."

"Yeah, but there's still your salary to consider."

"I'll more than earn my keep. Heck, I process more files than Billy Joe ever did, and I didn't even go to law school. I'll keep a record of my hours and the legal type work I do, not to mention keeping the books and greeting people, typing and everything, plus helping you when you go to court."

"Helping me when I go to court?"

Dixie rolled her eyes. "Of course, I would. Do you really believe I'd let you try a case all by yourself, do you?"

"Why would I need your help?"

"Are you kidding me? I've seen what you can do in court. Remember spilling the water—and in the court of appeals no less? Boy, that was a doozy."

Deloris' face heated up. "We were talking about your salary."

"You can pay me when the money comes in. Just like you get paid, see, I'll get paid only when a client ponies up. And trust me, I know how to get them to do it when they don't." Dixie smiled broadly. "Now, you gotta admit this is a durn good deal. I mean, you oughtta be glad you'll have a decent office with a telephone, secretary-bookkeeper, title searcher—a Miss Can-do-everything. And you'll have you a real investigator—a waiting room, for Pete's sake, and your own men's room. You won't have to be all time borrowing somebody else's—you know, like Kingry's Insurance or the motel down the street where they rent by the hour—or in some cases, the quarter hour. This way, you'll get out of your stupid truck and get some respect and not be a laughing stock around town. Oh yeah, I almost forgot. You'll have to quit giving away free ice water in the summertime too."

"I ain't about to give up my truck. I'll tell you that right now. It's my trademark. It's the best advertisement I got going."

"Some trademark."

Deloris remained silent for a moment, mulling over Billy Joe's offer and the way Dixie pitched it. "Let me give some thought to it, Dixie. I ain't one to jump into things, doncha know."

"Who you? Gimme a break." Dixie stared at Deloris. "Let me tell you something, Deloris. Give you a little free advice."

"What?"

"Don't you let yourself get bus-left."

"Bus-left?"

"Don't miss out on this opportunity. Make up your mind right now. Get on board. I don't know whether you are aware of this or not, but you're not the only lawyer in town who could use a helping hand and a durn good secretary in the bargain."

CHAPTER NINE

After several weeks behind a desk marred by the metal heel taps of Billy Joe Pratt's shoes, Deloris still missed his converted milk truck and the freedom it provided him. Whereas before, when he longed, for example, for a hotdog or cup of coffee from the Grease Pit, all he had to do was press the starter button on his truck and take off; but now he had to exit a building and walk to his truck. Worst of all, whenever he now left his office, he had to submit to a probing cross-examination by his secretary Dixie St. John concerning his precise destination or purpose for leaving and his expected return. Further, she would often raise additional questions about, among other things, when he would answer various letters, answer particular telephone calls, and draft certain documents.

His close, daily contact with the striking female whose work station sat right outside his private office sparked a subtle change in the feelings he had held for her before their close business relationship commenced, her physical attraction notwithstanding. He came to resent his being under her thumb and dependent on her to make a living, not only for himself but for the two of them—or the three of them, if Sergeant Unthank entered the picture.

But Deloris recognized he had only himself to blame for the situation, however unpleasant it could sometimes be. Better than anyone else, he knew Dixie had controlled Billy Joe, and thus he should have expected she would hold sway over him as well. Yet, he also recognized his relationship with Dixie had an upside. He made more money, and Dixie, although she lacked formal legal training, possessed a definite feel for the practice of law, a plus by any measure.

No sooner had Deloris opened the front door of the office building and entered the secretarial area than Dixie confronted him. "It's about time you got here," she said, her tone accusatory. "I tried calling you at your apartment and at the Grease Pit, but Glory said they hadn't seen you."

He stood staring at her, one hand to his hip. "What?"

"The solicitor's office called a while ago. They wanna hold Ginger's preliminary hearing this afternoon. Criminal court's coming up and they want the grand jury to act on the warrants, they said."

Deloris felt his muscles tense. He scratched his neck. "This afternoon?"

"Before a Judge Asdel."

"Don't know him. Never even heard of him, even."

"The woman told me he's the local magistrate and his filling station is in downtown Awenasa—"

" 'Downtown'? Awenasa's got a downtown? Heck, they don't even have a traffic light there, much less a downtown. It's just a—what?—just a place."

Dixie's eyes narrowed and she frowned. "I'm only telling you what she told me. She said come straight to Lot Granger Funeral home across the way. He uses one of their viewing rooms for a courtroom. You're to be there at three this afternoon, and they don't want you dragging it out neither because they've got a funeral starting at four o'clock, she said." Dixie laughed. "Oh yeah. One other thing. You're not supposed to pay any attention to the casket which'll be in the room. It'll have a woman in it. She'll be dead. The funeral home said they'll close it right before we get under way. We're not to worry about it."

"Durn it all, I hadn't expected them to hold a prelim so soon." His mind raced as he thought about what he must do to prepare for it. "Have you called—"

"I've already done that. I told Ginger you wanted her there no later than two-thirty." She looked at Deloris, her mouth tight. "You do want her there, don't you?"

"Why, of course I do."

"Ahead of time?"

"Yeah."

"But will thirty minutes give you enough time?"

"Yeah."

"Billy Joe, he'd usually wanted an hour to spend with a witness."

"Before a preliminary hearing?"

"He sure did."

"Well, that's Billy Joe. That ain't me."

"Have it your way."

"I will." Deloris opened the door to his private office. "I already know what they'll do. The judge'll have a law enforcement officer read a police report or maybe have one tell about questioning the prosecuting witness, and that'll be it, most likely. There'll be lots of hearsay, and after that the magistrate'll bind her over to the grand jury. It'll pretty much be a waste of time. You of all people ought to know that." He rolled his neck. "But who knows. We might learn something. Notice I said only 'we might,' I didn't say we would."

Deloris claimed his unopened mail on the edge of Dixie's desk and walked into his office.

***

Deloris crept along State Highway 711, looking for Lot Granger Funeral Home, the undertaker of choice for Democrats in Awenasa and surrounding areas. Republicans chose Kelley Mortuary and Chapel for the disposal of their human remains. Independents went to either.

"Isn't that it yonder?" Dixie said, pointing up ahead to a large white house across the road from a filling station whose Pepsi-Cola sign advertised it as Asdel's Oil and Gas and Magistrate's Office.

Deloris lifted his foot off the accelerator, applied the brakes, and made a turn into a long, circular drive that bordered the lawn of the funeral home, a red-roofed, clapboard building nestled beneath towering oak trees. A cemetery, parts of which dated back to the American Revolution, occupied the land to the right and rear of the old mansion. A paved parking area took up almost the whole left side.

"Yep, that's it," Deloris said.

Dixie pointed to the filling station. "So, the judge pumps gas for a living?"

"I guess so. I don't know anything about him," Deloris replied.

He motored up the drive in first gear. "Wonder if Ginger's made it here yet. I offered to come by and get her, but she said she had a way of getting here." He checked his watch. "It's still a little early. It's not but three twenty. We made it here a lot quicker than I thought we would."

He steered the truck into the first parking space in the parking lot. Before cutting the motor, he surveyed the area beyond the parking lot, noting the tombstones and vaults spread over the whole of the burial ground. Many appeared aged and weather-worn. Here and there lay an overturned tombstone.

Deloris took special notice of the large number of moss-covered oaks that grew throughout the cemetery and how they shaded the land below their canopies, providing cool havens to sun-baked bereaved during Greenfield's blistering summer months. A joke made the rounds that the devil used the hellish summers of the Greenfield area as a training ground for new demons. But now with November settling in and the temperatures dropping to cooler levels, the joke seemed out of place.

Dixie pointed a finger. "Look yonder, Deloris, at that obelisk. Whoever's buried below it must've been somebody real important. We got time. Since it's nice out, let's walk over there and see who it was. Want to? Might be somebody from the Revolution or a famous general or somebody like that. Wanna bet?"

Deloris and Dixie climbed out of the truck and sauntered over to inspect the gray stone pillar. An engraved granite slab with weathered, carved letters lay to the front of it. The inscription read, "Here lies the Honorable Bennie F. Whitecotton, Notary Public. Born January 27, 1820 and died July 7, 1874 of a gunshot wound suffered while leaving a wedding. His assailant, the cowardly Coy Bostic, later died of a broken neck when the floor on which he stood gave way."

Dixie pointed at the inscription. "Shot at a wedding. Now that's a story. Suppose it was his own?"

"I'd say so. Most likely, a disappointed suitor shot him."

"Or the bride's old man."

As Deloris turned around to head for the funeral home, he heard the sound of an approaching automobile. He looked toward the parking lot and watched a figure exit the car once it stopped and its engine quit. "Come on, Dixie," he said. "There's my client."

Ginger greeted Deloris and Dixie, and the three walked around to the front of the funeral home, conversing mainly about the splendor of the funeral home and how its exterior could not help but uplift a mourner's spirit no matter the depth of despair.

Once they stepped inside, however, gloom and sorrow took hold, deflating the uplifted spirit. They stood in a large room surrounded by the sound of piped-in religious music, the sugary scent of fresh flowers, and the display of framed prints of notable events in the life of Jesus, from his birth to his ascension. Tissue boxes and mints lay on every table and added to the funereal mood of the room.

Deloris elbowed Dixie. He pushed up his coat and shirt sleeves to show her his left arm. An array of goose bumps covered it. "Look here, Dixie, this place makes my skin crawl."

"May I help you, Sir and Ladies?" said a long-neck, wrinkled-face old man in a black suit, black vest, white shirt, and gray tie. "I'm Lot Granger, Sr., one of the owners."

Deloris extended his hand. "Yes, sir. I'm Lawyer Meek, Deloris Meek. We're here, me and these ladies, for a preliminary hearing that's supposed to take place in a little while."

"Oh, yes," Granger said. You need to go to Remembrance Room, the first room there on the right."

"Remembrance Room?" Deloris said.

"Yes. Years ago it used to be a music room. The piano that was there when this house was used as a residence, it's still in there and is in perfect tune. Would you believe it? Oh, to hear 'Rock of Ages' played upon it makes one long for eternal life. Yes, indeed."

None of the three responded.

"Oh, I better warn you. Each of our viewing rooms is occupied at the present time. So, I hope y'all won't mind having a hearing in a room where we have a loved one awaiting final rest."

Deloris shook his head. "We were told to expect that. We don't have a problem with it."

"Very good. Now, let's see, the Remembrance Room, who's sleeping in there? Oh yes, how could I forget? Miss Pauline. Miss Pauline—"

Deloris winked at Dixie and Ginger. "You're not serious are you, sir? Pauline's just sleeping?"

Granger laughed and clapped his hands as he led the way to the Remembrance Room. "Oh, you're sooooo funny, Mr. Meek. Oh, yes. Miss Pauline is very much asleep, but I'm afraid her slumber is—shall I say?—eternal. That is, sir, she is dead, very dead indeed, a state we all one day will experience." He leaned in close to Deloris and whispered, "But between me and thee, I believe poor Miss Pauline's been dead for a long, long time, if you get my meaning?" Granger bit his lip and raised and lowered his shoulders.

The four entered the viewing room.

Granger tiptoed over to the casket and peered at the deceased, stroking his chin as he did so. He shook his head as he frowned. "Yes, she's dead, bless her heart. Come look at the way we have her prepared. She looks absolutely beautiful. And I hate to say this, but it is certainly true. She looks much better now than she ever did before. We pride ourselves on our ability to do this. Know what her brother said about her when he visited her this morning? Said she looks so different they might not've recognized her when she arrived in heaven." Granger snorted with laughter, its harsh sound resembling one made by a pig.

"That brother of hers. They threw away the mold when they made him. Yes, they did, they did. Do you know him? His nickname is 'Chip.' Know why? He's a potato chip inspector at the potato chip factory in Greenfield. If he's around, you can't miss him, he's so huge. I do believe he eats all the discards he—"

"Excuse me, Mr. Granger." Deloris looked at his watch. "What time will Judge Asdel get here? We're already a little past what I thought was the time for the hearing to start."

Granger put a hand to his mouth. "Ahhh, what time will he get here? That depends on when he gets through with whatever he's doing. Sometimes, we've had to wait until he finishes changing oil in a car or fixing a flat tire or whatever."

Deloris looked around the room. All he saw were the casket with Miss Pauline in repose, several rows of chairs, a few flowers, and a piano. "Does the judge have any desks for himself and the lawyers, Mr. Granger? Can I help you bring them in here?"

Granger's mouth opened, and he shook his head. "Oh, no, no, no. You see, what he does is he'll take one of those chairs on the front row and place it there in front of the casket—that is, when we've got one in here. The chair will be used by the witnesses when they testify. The judge'll turn it around so it'll face all the others—you know, those in which the mourners usually sit when they come in here to view the body. The lawyers and their clients, they'll usually occupy the front row. Everybody else, they'll sit behind them. Personally, in my humble opinion, it's a nice setup. It's a whole lot better than these storage rooms some of the magistrates use. I hear tell one of them uses a barn, can you imagine that? A barn, mind you. I think were I a lawyer I'd prefer a corpse to a pig any old day."

Dixie grunted. "Depends on the pig."

"Beg pardon, Missy?" Granger said as he bent over Miss Pauline's coffin and straightened the collar on her gown.

Deloris shook his head at Dixie as a reproof.

As Granger faced the three again, Deloris smiled at Granger. "Let me ask you this, sir. What about the judge? Where does he sit?"

"Judge Asdel? Oh, he doesn't sit—never does. After we close the casket—that is, when we have a casket—"

"I got the picture," Deloris says, interrupting. "Y'all'll close Miss Pauline's casket, and he'll go stand behind it, I'm guessing."

Granger's lips puckered. "Yes, that's right. But I'm sure Miss Pauline won't mind, won't mind at all. She wasn't the type who'd stick her nose into somebody else's business when she was alive, and she certainly wouldn't do it now that she's gone to glory. No way would she interfere with a court hearing. No, indeed." He snorted. "Judge Asdel is used to having a deceased present during his hearings. Sometimes I wonder if he doesn't purposely schedule them when he knows we'll have a departed loved one in the viewing room. Could be, I suppose, he believes having one in attendance will somehow induce good behavior on the part of all those participating."

Deloris scratched his nose. "I don't get it, Mr. Granger."

Granger raised his chin and intoned, "In my humble opinion, the presence of the dead constitutes a subtle reminder to us all that one day we will each one face an ultimate justice when all will be revealed. Indeed, every courtroom in the land should display a casket for that very reason. But alas, that could never happen. No, never. We have enough trouble as it is simply asking permission to post one of our calendars." He lowered his head and shook it.

"Oh well," the undertaker said, touching his cheek. "Want me to tell you something? I don't remember a single time when the judge has ever had to call somebody down." He snorted. "Maybe they ought to put a dead body in every courtroom. Might make folks behave better. That judge, he's a most clever person, especially for a mechanic." He paused. "But oh, his hands. Always dirty looking. Grease caked under his fingernails. Ugh! I wish you'd look at them when he comes in."

Granger withdrew a handkerchief from a hind pocket and wiped his mouth. "I do wish he would get here, though. Sometimes, we've had to delay a funeral service because one of these hearings will drag on and on and on. You lawyers, some of you anyway, and I'll excuse present company, don't seem to know when to quit. They have what my daddy referred to as 'diarrhea of the mouth.' Excuse me, ladies."

Granger touched Deloris on his upper arm. He immediately brushed Granger's hand away.

"Only kidding," Granger said. "No offense intended. I'm not talking about you, sir. I'm sure you're not like that. Not you, sir." He looked at Dixie and Ginger. "Is he, ladies?"

Deloris did not give the two women an opportunity to respond. "Well, Mr. Granger," he said "if you will excuse us, I gotta talk to my client for a few minutes. You know, before the judge gets here. Okay?"

Troubles and Kuddles

Granger raised both hands. "Of course. Of course." He bowed. "If you good people will excuse me, I'll be running along. If you need anything, merely give us, as they say, a holler—but don't holler too loud, now. You wouldn't want to wake the dead, now would you?" He snorted. 'If you did that, we'd have to issue a refund, and we wouldn't want to do that." He snorted again.

After Granger exited the viewing room and closed the double doors of the room behind him, Deloris showed Ginger and Dixie to seats on the first row of the stand of chairs. All three seated themselves.

"Ginger, I know we've talked before. Is there anything else I need to know? Anything you've meant to tell me but forgot to? Have you heard anything, remembered anything at all?"

Ginger dropped her head. "No, I can't say I have. There isn't much to tell. Like I told you when we first talked about this, I rode out there, I saw Kuddles, and when I didn't see anyone else out there, I put her in the car, and brought her on back home with me. I figured he left her there for me, knowing I'd come."

Deloris nodded and scratched beneath his eye

Ginger went on. "Next thing I know, here come the police with a search warrant, and they arrest me and take me and Kuddles downtown. They say I shot at Brother Holcomb and stole Kuddles from him. But I didn't do it. You know, shoot at Brother Holcomb. Now, I did take Kuddles and bring her to my place. I admit that. I couldn't bear to leave her out there all by her lonesome, now could I? Anyway, I don't even own a gun, and never have. Plus, I wouldn't even know how to shoot one if I did."

Before Deloris could make further inquiry, the doors to the viewing room flew open. Deloris turned to his left to see a dumpy woman with a man's hair style stomp into the room and make a beeline for the casket, using the foulest of language as she went. A tall, dignified male wearing a dark suit with shinny elbows followed close behind her, a hat in his hand and a trail of dandruff flakes in his wake. Neither the woman nor the man appeared to notice Deloris and his two companions.

As she stood viewing the decease, the woman jammed her hands to her hips. The man stepped beside her and stood silent, his arms crossed in front.

"Hot damn!" the woman suddenly exclaimed. "I knowed it'd happen! I just knowed it would! I knowed it, I knowed it, I knowed it! I oughtta be a damn fortuneteller. These damn Democrats." She glared at the man beside her. "I told you we should've had the Republican one do her, but nooooo, you insisted on these folks. Damn communists, if you ask me. That's what they are."

The man leaned toward the woman and stretched his neck. "What, Inez? Something wrong, baby?"

"Hell yeah, there's something wrong. These damn Democrats of yours, they done stole Mama's wedding band. Tell me. You see it on her finger? Do you? Well, do you?"

"Why no, I don't. But how you know they stole it, sweet?"

"How? Cause I put it on her finger last night my ownself, that's how, and it's gone and they're Democrats."

"And you think one of them here done it, hon?"

"Hell yes I do, cause I come by here after choir practice—I told you we'd started our Christmas cantata. Anyway, they were getting ready to close up shop and turn the lights off when I got here, but they let me come in to put her ring back on—we'd taken it off at the hospital, remember? Soon as I done that, I left and went on out to my car. By the time I'd backed outta the parking space, they'd done turned the lights off on the porch and inside the front of building. There wasn't nobody here when I got here but me and them who run this damn place, the damn Democrats.

"If you got a little money, the damn Democrats, they wanna take it from you so they can give it to somebody else after they get their cut, the bastards. They're all alike. I call them the 'Gimmethats.' Sure they took it. I wasn't born yesterday."

The woman whipped around, hands still to her hips, and stared at Dixie.

"Don't look at me," Dixie said, throwing up her hands. "I sure as heck didn't take it off her."

The woman squinted at Deloris, her lips pursed.

Dixie laughed and angled her head toward Deloris. "You know something, you just might better search him. He's not only a lawyer, he's a Democrat—a big time, double-dipped, capital 'D' one."

Deloris jumped up from his seat. "Dixie, mind what you say to this lady here. This is no laughing matter." He smiled at the woman. "Pay no attention to her, ma'am. She's my secretary, and she's just making a little joke. We're just here for a hearing. It's supposed to get under way in a few minutes, least I hope it will."

"A hearing?"

"Yessum. It's a court-type hearing—you know, one with a judge and all," Deloris said.

The woman turned and shook a finger at the casket behind her. "My poor ol' mama is laying there dead and somebody's done swiped her wedding band off her finger and my heart's breaking to pieces and y'all can sit there and make little jokes and not give the dead the respect they're entitled to?" She gave Dixie a look, her eyes again in a squint and her lips once more pursed.

"Well, Blondi," the woman said to Dixie in an apparent dig at her peroxide hair, "were you joking about him taking Mama's ring or did you really see him take it off her?" The woman balled her fists and held them in front of Dixie's face. "Tell me the truth. And you *will* tell me the truth, even if I gotta beat it outta you. And I can do it too, by jiminy, and if you don't believe me, ask him." She jerked a thumb toward the man with her. He coiled away a foot or two, gritting his teeth.

For the first time he could remember, Deloris saw genuine fright manifested in Dixie's face. It had taken on a dark red color that overcame the makeup she wore. He speculated Dixie may have felt she'd finally met her match.

Dixie rose from her seat and faced the woman. Dixie stood a good foot higher than she. Dixie smiled. "Ma'am, I don't know why I said what I did. I'm sorry. I guess I was only trying to make things a little bit livelier in here. I am sorry. No, he didn't take anything off her. We're sorry for your loss, truly we are." Dixie's chin fell to her bosom.

The woman waggled a finger at Dixie. "I tell you one thing, if you were my secretary, I'd fire your butt for what you done just now. I sure would. You should be ashamed of yourself." The woman paused. "And why come you got on so much makeup for? Ain't you never read *First Timothy*, 2:9? You look like a damn harlot."

"Why thank you," Dixie replied. "And you, ma'am, you—"

"I heard loud talk," Lot Granger said upon reentering the room. "Morning, Miss Inez. Hiram. Is there something wrong in here?"

"Just a slight case of robbery, that's all," Inez said. "Somebody lifted Mama's wedding ring clean off of her finger. I put it on her last night my ownself. That's why come I was here last night. Don't you remember?"

Granger opened his mouth to speak, but the woman shushed him before his words could come.

She gave Dixie a dirty look. "See that made-up woman right there, she first told me that big dumb-looking fella she's with was the one took it, and now she says no, he ain't done no such a thing. I dunno what to believe, with her talking outta both sides of that painted mouth of hers. Look at her, the trashy thing."

Granger again tried to speak, but the woman stopped him.

"You just shut up while I'm talking. I'm telling y'all this, me and Hiram, we ain't about to leave this room till Mama's ring is back on her finger, and after it's put back, we want a padlock put on the coffin. Hell, what with all these lawyers and Gimmethat-Democrats hanging about and creeping all around like a den of thieves, it's a damn wonder they ain't toted off everything y'all got in here, including the embalming table, the piano, and all them folding chairs."

"Please, Miss Inez—"

"I'll tell you what'll please me. Go call the police, why don't you? Not that it'll do any good to call the sorry things. All they do is eat donuts and skeet tobacco juice. No wonder they're so fat and outta shape." Inez paused to catch her breath. "But I don't reckon there's any need to call them. Those nincompoops never do catch anybody for stealing. If they ever did, the celebration that'd follow, why it'd rival that'un they held on V-J Day after we showed the Japs a thing or two."

Granger smiled and closed his eyes. "Now, Miss Inez," he said, his head turned slightly and finally able to get a word in edgewise, "don't you know us any better than that? After you left here last night, I happened to notice the ring. To reduce the chance of somebody coming in here and stealing it, I myself removed it and put it away for safekeeping. That's a standing policy we have. I didn't anticipate you'd be here so soon this afternoon. Come on with me. I'll show you where I put it last night. Okay?" Granger stepped to the side and held out his arm. "This way, Miss Inez. You, too, Hiram."

Once the three exited the viewing room, Deloris, still standing and his arms folded against his chest shook his head as he looked at Dixie. "Have you lost your mind?"

Dixie laughed. "Oh, relax, Deloris."

"Relax? Let me tell you something—"

"Morning, everybody," came a voice to Deloris' right. It belonged to Judge Asdel, a man of average height in a pair of greasy white overalls. A uniformed deputy sheriff, who carried a folder, followed the magistrate inside the room. The deputy selected a seat on the first row near the door, plopped onto the black, metal chair, and stretched out. He greeted Deloris with a slight nod and a weak smile.

The magistrate approached Deloris, his right hand extended. Deloris stood and took hold of it. "Good morning, Your Honor. I'm Deloris Meek." He gestured toward Ginger. "I represent Miss Childree here. The other lady's my secretary, Miss St. John."

The magistrate glanced at Ginger, but gave Dixie a little more of his attention, his Adam's apple bobbing as he ogled her. Deloris thought he heard Asdel say the given name of Christ beneath his breath.

"Okay," Judge Asdel said, turning around. "I see they didn't close the casket like they're supposed to. He stepped over to the casket and smiled at the deceased. "And a pleasant good morning to you, ma'am. Hope you had a restful night. If you don't mind, I'm gonna close you out for a little bit. This won't take long, so don't get your nose all out of joint. I'll put you back on display in a few minutes, you lovely thing you. Just take you a little snooze while we have our hearing." He closed the casket and tiptoed behind it. "All right, Deputy Perry. Come on around and take you a seat. But before you do, let me swear you as a witness."

The deputy, an older, balding man with horn-rim glasses, shifted the file folder from his right hand to his left as he went forward. After administration of the oath, he seated himself and crossed his legs at the ankles. He smiled at Deloris who smiled back.

"You're a deputy, aren't you?" the magistrate said.

"Yes, sir. Been one eighteen year come December 10. Name's Lester Perry, Jr. Most folks, though, they call me Junior."

"All right, Junior it is." The magistrate smiled. "Junior, tell me this, did you have you a chance here lately to go investigate a shooting a little outside Awenasa?"

"Yes, sir. At a picnic area on Belle's Highway." Perry opened the file folder. "A man who said he was Dr. James Holcomb—he ain't no medical kinda doctor but one of 'em preacher kind—you know, a 'vangelist—he come by the office 'bout two o'clock, or close to it. This was, on—let me see here." Perry withdrew a paper and read it, holding the paper close to his face. "It was on Wednesday, September 2, 1970. He filed a complaint. Told us this person he called Ginger Childree drove out to this picnic spot where he'd stop at to eat him a baloney sandwich and drank him an ice-cold Dr. Pepper he bought after he filled up with gas. Said he brought his 'triloquist dummy' long with him and had it sittin' on one of 'em benches they got out there. Said he uses the dummy a whole lot in his ministry. He called it 'Cruddles' or 'Puddles'—somethin' like that. Ain't sure."

" 'Kuddles,' " Ginger called out.

Everyone, frowning, turned and looked at Ginger.

"I'm sorry, Your Honor," she said, dropping her head.

The magistrate ignored her. "Continue, Junior."

"Yes, sir. Let me see here. Anyway, he said he 'cided he'd walk down into the woods. Said he left his dummy sittin' there on

Troubles and Kuddles

the bench. Said the Childree woman was 'posed to meet him there to talk over some business of some kind. He didn't say what. Said while he was down there in the woods, the Childree woman, she come drivin' up and got outta her car and took a shot at him. Said he took off runnin', and he run till he plumb give out and waited way, way back there in the woods for near 'bout thirty or forty minutes, hidin' 'hind a tree. Said he run away cause he was 'fraid she'd take 'nother shot at him. Said he finally sneaked on back to the picnic area and when he got back there he seen right off his dummy wasn't nowhere to be found and the woman who'd shot at him, she done hightailed it outta there. That's when he got in his car and come on to Greenfield to the sheriff's office to let us know what'd happened."

The deputy paused. "Y'all ain't got no ice water, have you?"

The magistrate pointed to Dixie. "Pretty lady, you mind running and getting Deputy Perry a glass of water?"

Dixie stood. "Have I gotta run to go get it?"

The magistrate blushed. "Oh, no ma'am. Walking's fine. We'll wait till you get back before we do anything else. Thank you, ma'am."

Dixie left the room and returned with a glass of water within less than two minutes. The deputy emptied it in a single gulp.

"Go on, Deputy Perry with what you were telling us."

The deputy nodded. "Yes, sir. Later on, we found out where the Childree woman lived at. You give us a search warrant, and we went and served it there at her apartment."

Perry dug through the file folder and withdrew two blue papers. "These here, they're the search warrant you give us, Your Honor, and the whatchacallit we turned in after we got done servin' the warrant on her. Deputy Eddie Little, he went with me. He'd've come this mornin', but he took sick and didn't come on duty. Got the trots. His wife, she called to let us know. Said he had 'em real bad. Said he'd durn near wore out the carpet in the hallway goin' back and forth to the toilet.

"But goin' back to us servin' the search warrant, when we started to go through her place, we found what looked to us like the doctor's dummy—you know, the one what the warrant said to be on the lookout for. I left Deputy Little with Miss Childree and took the dummy to the doctor to see if it was the right one, if he recognized it. He said it was the one, all right. I let him have it back, and he give me a receipt for it. It should be in the file here. Wanna see it?"

Judge Asdel shook his head. "I don't think we need to do that. We'll take your word for it." He gestured for Perry to resume his testimony.

"Okay. When I left him, that's when I went on back to her place and 'rested her for shootin' at the preacher and stealin' his dummy. She denied shootin' at him or stealin' his dummy. But there it was when we got there, Your Honor, sittin' right there in her livin' room, plain as day, grinnin' at us." He closed the file folder. "That's 'bout all I know, Judge, Your Honor."

"Thank you, Junior," Judge Asdel said. "All right, Mr. Meek, if you wanna, I'm gonna let you question the deputy. But there ain't no need to go deep into it. There's probable cause here, and if you're any kind of a lawyer at all, you know there is and I ain't got no choice but to let the grand jury pass on it. So, go on and question him a little bit, but please don't go on a long time cause if you do I'll have to cut you off, although I don't wanna have to do that. You see, I got me some cars over there at my place across the highway to service and all. Okay?"

Deloris rose from his seat. "Officer, did you know Dr. Holcomb?"

"Heard tell of him, that's 'bout it."

"What'd you hear?"

"Not much. That's he some kinda tent preacher, out doin' the Lord's work. That's 'bout it. Mama and Daddy, they raised me Lutheran. We ain't much into tent preachers. I ain't faultin' 'em what do go to one of 'em, understand. But me and my folks, we just didn't never do it, see."

"So, you're not familiar with Dr. Holcomb's reputation for truth and—and what's that other word?" Deloris paused a moment.

"Veracity. You familiar with the reverend's reputation for truth and veracity?"

"No, sir. Not no neither one."

"So, whether he told you the truth, you don't have any idea at all, do you?"

"No, sir. Sure don't. All I done while ago is tell you what he told me, what we done, and what she said later on. That's it."

"Anything else you can tell us about your investigation into this matter, Deputy?"

"No, sir. I done told it all."

"You say Deputy Little went with you to serve the search warrant?"

"Yes, sir. He'd been here except, like I told y'all, his wife says he's got the trots."

"Anybody other than Deputy Little help in any way with the investigation?"

"No, sir. Like I say, him and me, we found the dummy we 'posed to been lookin' for at her place."

"And she told you she didn't steal it, that she found it there on one of the benches, and didn't see Holcomb anyplace, right?"

"And she brung it on back home with her. Right."

"Thank you, deputy."

Before Perry could stand, Dixie stood. "Excuse me, Judge, could I make a suggestion to Mr. Meek. Won't take me but a sec."

Judge Perry chuckled. "Why sure thing, honey." He waved his hand. "Go right ahead." He crossed his arms and grinned.

Dixie walked in front of Ginger and whispered to Deloris whose face shown beet red. Although embarrassed because of her interference, he listened to what she had to say.

Deloris took two steps toward the witness, mainly to get away from Dixie. "Your Honor, one more question of the officer, if I may?"

"Yes, sir. One more, and that's it. I'm taking you at your word, counselor. Remember what I said about what all I got waiting across the highway. I'd asked you to cut it short, remember."

Deloris nodded his acknowledgment of the magistrate's request. "Deputy, was Holcomb told to be here for this hearing? You know, notified of this hearing?"

The deputy looked around at the magistrate. "I dunno. I didn't do it. Judge?"

"Yes," the magistrate said, "we mailed him a notice. Oh, wait a second. He called me. I most forgot. He wanted to know if it was all that important for him to come. I told him no, that lots of times, the arresting officer, he'd handle everything. He said, good 'cause the time I'd set for the hearing was the time him and the Lord were in the habit of getting together for conversation and he didn't want to disappoint the Lord by not showing up." He paused. "So, yeah, Mr. Meek, we give Dr. Holcomb notice of this hearing, but he had him a good enough reason for not coming.

"To be honest, though, whether a prosecuting witness'll come or not, it ain't all that important, not at this stage, it ain't. Even if I dismissed all the charges, the prosecutor, he could still go after an indictment from the grand jury. And you've practice law long enough, I suspect, to know that and also know them grand juries, they pretty much'll do whatever the prosecutor wants done."

The magistrate patted the top of the coffin. "Thank y'all, Officer Perry and Mr. Meek." He smiled at Dixie. "You too, ma'am. I find there's probable cause. The defendant is bound over to the grand jury on both charges, assault with intent to kill and robbery. We stand adjourned."

He moved around to the front of the casket and propped its lid open. "There, Miss Pauline, you sweet thing," he said smiling at the corpse, "that didn't take us too long, now did it? You sure do look mighty, mighty pretty, laying there, all dolled up, ready to catch the Beulah train. You look like an angel, you sure do. I expect they'll have you outta here before too long. Make sure now, you don't get on the wrong train. That Black Diamond Express, it goes the other way, see, and it's always real, real crowded—standing room only, they say. So, be careful, you hear? Watch what you're doing."

***

Ginger joined Deloris and Dixie in the parking lot of the funeral home where Deloris had set two folding chairs beneath the canopy of a pecan tree. He sat in the doorway of one of the two back doors of his truck.

"I know you've got to get on back to the bottling plant, Ginger," Deloris said, "but like I told you inside I need to talk to you about something that doesn't have anything to do with charges against you here."

Ginger crossed her legs. "You've got me curious, Mr. Meek."

"It's about Wally, that is, Eli—Eli Fromberg."

Ginger gave Deloris a studied look.

"This fella come by to talk to me about Wally. His name is Jade Ziglar—"

"Jade Ziglar?"

"Yeah. He's a private investigator from up north—New Jersey, he said. He's been looking for Wally. Frankly, I'm kinda curious about him—Wally, I mean. If you don't mind telling me, what all can you tell me about him, stuff you might've learned about his life and so forth. I'm especially interested in anything you might've learned about him after you left him in Shreveport and went with Holcomb."

Ginger nodded but said nothing for a few moments.

"Why are you 'kinda curious,' as you put it?"

Deloris sighed. "Okay, this is what I've been told. Wally's had this rich uncle. Somebody shot him there in his house—the man's house. There wasn't any sign of a break-in or struggle of any kind. Whoever shot him, shot him in the back of his head—meaning it wasn't no suicide. He died, leaving a lot of money and property—millions of dollars' worth, Ziglar says.

"Well, Wally, he's the closest kin. In other words, he stands to inherit all his uncle had. So, naturally, he became a suspect. The police, they're looking for him. Now, if he did kill his uncle, he couldn't inherit anything and other folks, they would get what the old man owned—you know, his estate. That's why come Ziglar's looking for him. He represents the bank that's the executor of the estate, and they wanna make durn sure whoever they give the money and everything to that they're the ones supposed to get it, doncha see."

"Wally kill somebody? No way."

"I left out one detail," Deloris said. "Wally was the last person seen with his uncle. Some people saw them together earlier that same evening, dining together."

Ginger remained silent as in thought, gazing at the branches above her head.

Deloris continued. "I have to tell you, Ginger, his roaming all over the country doesn't look good for him. Some might consider it hiding out—you know, on the run, so to speak."

Ginger uncrossed her legs and pulled at the hem of her dress. "Wally is no killer, Mr. Meek. To tell you the truth, I'm not comfortable talking about him, not in any sort of negative way. Ever since I left him in Shreveport and joined Brother Holcomb's ministry, I've been torn about leaving Wally like I did and him hurt from the beating he took, not to mention seeing Kody get torn all to pieces. You saw what happened and know what I did, leaving him all alone and hurt."

"Saw what happened? Heck, I was part of what happened."

"Yes, you were."

"And I left him too. Forget all that right now. What could you tell me that might help him?" Deloris asked.

"I don't know all that much about him. He's a real private person. I know he's from New Jersey, from a place called Beverly. He attended Rutgers for a while, but I don't know for how long. I know he didn't graduate. I do know that. The Army drafted him, and he landed in Special Services doing his ventriloquist act. He always laughed about his Army career, saying he fought communism with a dummy." Ginger laughed. "On the other hand, he said, a whole lot of other people did the same thing. You know, fought communism with a dummy. He said the only difference was their dummies were called 'sergeants.' "

Deloris laughed. Dixie didn't.

"How'd he happen to learn ventriloquism anyway?" Deloris asked.

Troubles and Kuddles

"About all I know is he said his parents bought him a 'Charlie McCarthy' look-alike for his birthday—his fourteenth, I believe he said. He ordered him some books on ventriloquism and started practicing throwing his voice when he was in junior high school. He bought him some other dummies—even made some. Finally, he landed an appearance on a kid's show at a TV station when he was at Rutgers, and that's when he left there. And right when he got started good, the Army drafted him."

"Did he ever talk about his family?"

"His folks—his mama and daddy, they'd been killed in a bus accident. It ran off a cliff someplace in Europe, killed them and ten or twelve others."

"That's terrible," Dixie said.

"How old was he when that happened?" Deloris asked.

"Sixteen or seventeen," Ginger said. "He was in high school at the time, best I remember."

"Who took care of him after that?"

"His mama's brother. I don't think he ever told me his name or where he lived or anything. If he did, I don't recall it. I assume it was New Jersey."

"Does the name Izzy or Isadore Goldmann ring a bell?"

"No," Ginger said, shaking her head.

"Has he told you what he's been doing since Shreveport?"

"Only he had a hard time finding work because he had never trained to do anything but ventriloquism. Because he lost some teeth and had busted lips because of that airman assaulting him like he did there at the nightclub that night, it was not until way later he could do ventriloquist work. He had to get his teeth replaced, and it was hard getting used to the bridge, especially being able to do ventriloquism with it. He said he practiced and practiced every night after work, hours at a time."

"What kinda work did he do?"

"You name it. He said he's done it. He said once even drove a milk truck." Ginger smiled at Deloris. "Said it kinda've reminded him of you when he did that."

"Did he—"

Dixie interrupted. "Ginger—excuse me, Deloris—but doesn't it strike you as a little bit strange now that you know he had him a rich uncle that Wally didn't stay there with him and let him help him till he got back on his feet? Why would he work in those low-paying jobs when he may could've gotten help from a well-to-do uncle? Doesn't make sense to me."

"I dunno. Wally is an independent sort. Maybe that's why. Anyway, I don't know what his relationship was with his uncle. I dunno if they got along or not. He never talked about him other than he had an uncle who took him in after his parents got killed."

"Was there ever any sign Wally had a temper? You know, would he lose his cool or do violent things, especially if things didn't go his way?" Deloris asked.

"No, never. I have to say, Wally is one of the sweetest, most thoughtful people I have ever known. I never once saw him get angry. Even when we'd do our act and get heckled, he'd fire back at the hecklers, but he wasn't mad at them or anything. He understood heckling was a part of show business. He practiced and practiced come-backs, a lot of them he bought from joke writers."

Deloris scratched his neck. "You know, you say that, but his dummy—"

"Kody," Ginger said.

"Yeah, Kody. His personality was the opposite of Wally's. He could be smart-mouthed, insulting, crude even. And he'd be that way even when he wasn't performing or even when—and this is what's weird—even when Wally was carrying him around in a case."

Ginger waved her hand. "Oh, that was simply an act, Mr. Meek."

"An act?"

"Yes. I got to doing it too. We'd do it merely to see how people would react. We thought it a lot of fun."

"Y'all did it to me one time. Remember the first motel we stopped at after I picked y'all up? I thought . . . well, never mind. Do you know whether he owned a gun?"

"I wouldn't know if he did. All I can say is I never saw him with one, and I never even heard him speak about owning one either."

"And you never heard him mention his uncle Izzy Goldmann?"

"I don't recall if he ever did. I just remember he told me he'd lived with an uncle for a while after his parents got killed."

***

Sergeant Unthank greeted Deloris and Dixie upon their returned to the office from Awenasa.

"Deloris, I tried to catch you before you left the funeral home, but they told me you'd been long gone."

"What?" Deloris said as Dixie went behind her desk and sat in front of her typewriter.

"Two things," Unthank said. "First, the solicitor's office telephoned to say the solicitor has set the date for Ginger's trial. It's a month from today. Said it'd be the first case called for trial after they get through processing the guilty pleas."

"A month from today? All right. And the other thing?"

"Wally Teal is on his way here to see you."

Unthank looked up at the office clock. It read eight-fifteen.

"He should be here in a few minutes," Unthank said, "that is, if he left when he said he would."

"What's he want, did he say?" Deloris asked in a soft voice.

"No, sir."

Deloris also checked the time, both with his watch and the clock on the wall. "You didn't ask?"

"I did, but he still wouldn't say."

All of a sudden, the door opened and in walked Wally Teal.

"Good evening, Mr. Meek," he said, his hand held out for Deloris to shake. "I'm glad I caught you. He nodded to Dixie. "You too, Miss Dixie."

"Yeah, long time, no see."

As Wally and Deloris shook hands, Wally smiled at Unthank.

"And you, sir, must be Sergeant Unthank," Wally said recovering his hand. "Thank you, sir, for arranging for me to see Mr. Meek without an appointment tonight."

Unthanked smiled. "I really didn't arrange anything, Mr. Teal."

Dixie twirled a sheet of paper into her typewriter carriage. "I can't tell you, Wally, how many appointments Deloris did not have to cancel to be able to talk with you this evening. They number in the hundreds."

Deloris, ignoring the cut, opened the door to his office and stood beside it. "Come on in, Wally, and take a seat. Pay her no attention."

Before the two men entered Deloris' private office, Wally paused and said, "Mr. Meek, thank you for seeing me. I know it's late and after office hours, but I just had to talk to you, sir."

Deloris nodded and patted Wally on his back before following him into his office. He offered Wally one of the two chairs in front of his desk. Deloris assumed the other one.

Once settled, the two men engaged in some small talk brought to a close when Deloris inquired about the purpose for Teal's after-hours visit.

Wally sat with his brow wrinkled. "Mr. Meek," he said in a soft voice, "Ginger called me after her hearing this afternoon and told me you said a man had been asking around about me. Who's he?"

"His name is Jaden Ziglar. Goes by Jade. He says he's a private investigator from New Jersey."

"And he's investigating me?"

"The police are too."

"Yes, sir."

"Did you know your uncle was dead?"

"Yes, sir."

"Know he'd been murdered?"

"Yes, sir."

"And you stand to inherit millions?"

Wally blinked and his mouth dropped open. "No, sir. Millions, you say?"

"Did you know you were the last person seen with him before he got murdered?"

Wally did not respond.

"You and him, y'all were seen together shortly before he got killed. Y'all were having dinner. This apparently makes you a prime suspect."

Wally nodded. "Yes, sir." He clasped his hands, dropped them between his legs, and leaned forward, staring at the floor.

"Well, Wally, what about it?" Deloris said. "Care to say anything?"

He raised his head. "This is a bit overwhelming. You know, my inheriting his estate."

"Only a bit?"

"Well, a whole lot."

"Let's cut to the chase. Did you kill your uncle? And before you answer, you can tell me as your lawyer."

"No way, Mr. Meek would I ever do anything like that."

Deloris nodded. "Uh-huh. Know who might've done it?"

"No, sir."

"Where'd you go after y'all had dinner that evening?"

"That's when I left town to go and try to find Ginger."

"When did you learn of your uncle's murder?"

Wally did not answer right away. "I guess maybe a week later. I read about it in the paper."

"You didn't return home?"

"No, because the news article said the police were looking for me. Only they referred to me by my real name and not by my stage name—you know, Wally Teal. I got scared. That's why I didn't go back. The paper said, like you've pointed out, I was last person known to have been seen with him that night. I put two and two together and figured they thought I did it. I'm not stupid."

Wally inhaled. "Another thing, and I expect the police know all about this. He and I argued there in the restaurant. Our argument attracted the attention of some of the patrons and the staff. One of the waiters, he came over to the table and asked us to, you know, kinda hold it down or leave the premises."

"What did y'all argue about?"

"I told him I wanted to get back into show business and hopefully find Ginger so we might resurrect our act. He wouldn't hear of it. He wanted me to go back to college and apply to law school after I got an undergraduate degree. I didn't want to be a lawyer, and I still don't. No offense, Mr. Meek."

"Is that all y'all talked about or argued about?"

Wally exhaled. "One other thing, but it wasn't important. It had to do with my personal life, which I didn't want to talk about with him—or with anybody else for that matter. I prefer to deal with the situation in my own way. The main argument—the one that caused the waiter to come to our table—it was his objection to me not wanting to return to school. In fact, after the waiter walked over, I left the restaurant, went by the house, packed me a few of my things, and hit the road. I wasn't about to spend another night there."

"You say you left and went by the house. I guess you mean your uncle's?"

"Yes, sir. Only he wasn't there. I left before he got back home."

A quiet settled about the room. Deloris rubbed the back of his neck. "Wally, I've got some advice for you, but you won't like it."

Wally's eyes met those of Deloris. "I can kinda guess what you're gonna say, Mr. Meek."

"And what's that, Wally?"

"That I turn myself in."

"I wouldn't phrase it like that. As far as I know, all the police wanna do is talk to you. If there is an arrest warrant out for you, I don't know anything about it. Ziglar didn't say anything about there being one. So, yeah, you should contact the police and tell them you're available to talk to them and wanna help them find out who killed your uncle. Besides, if Ziglar is who he says he is, it'd be my guess he's already told the police where they might could find you."

"You think so, Mr. Meek?"

"Sure do. But irregardless, you need to clear this thing up. There might could be something in what you tell them which could aid their investigation and help them find out who really did kill your uncle, doncha see."

Wally stood and looked toward the door. "Well, let me think on it some. Thank you for talking to me tonight, sir."

Before Deloris could stand to shake Wally's hand goodbye, Wally had bolted from the room.

A moment later Dixie appeared in the doorway. "What in the world was that all about? He shot out of here like he'd been fired from a cannon."

"It's a long story. He apparently didn't like the advice I gave him."

CHAPTER TEN

On the mid-November morning scheduled for Ginger Childree's trial on charges of assault with intent to kill and armed robbery and with Dixie St. John beside him in the passenger seat, Deloris drove his converted milk truck into the parking lot of the county courthouse. He selected a parking space at the rear of the courthouse. His client, who sat on a sun-lit bench next to the sidewalk near the back steps of the courthouse, stood as Deloris pulled to a stop. Dixie and Deloris exited the truck and joined her at the bench.

"Morning, Ginger," Deloris said, motioning her to sit. He turned to Dixie. "See if you can find me some coffee over yonder at that café across the street while I talk a little bit to Ginger. Okay?"

Dixie made a face but walked away without verbal comment, her light winter jacket draped over her arm.

Deloris took a seat beside Ginger on the bench. "Ginger, we don't have much time. I talked to the solicitor's office last night. They've offered you a plea deal. We need to talk about it."

"You said they'd do that."

Deloris sighed. "Well, this is what they said. If you will plead guilty to a lesser-included charge within the indictment, which would be grand larceny, they said they'll dismiss the assault and robbery counts and recommend to the judge he give you a suspended sentence conditioned on you serving a year of probation. I even talked to them about letting you plead to petty larceny, but they wouldn't go along with that. They've discussed all this with Brother Holcomb, and he told them he's willing to go along with whatever they wanna do." Deloris swallowed. "I have to say, it sounds like a good deal to me. But it's your decision, of course."

Ginger sat in stunned silence. "But, Mr. Meek, I didn't do anything wrong. Why should I plead guilty to something I didn't do? I didn't steal Kuddles. I took her, yeah. But I didn't steal her"

Deloris nodded. "Trouble is, Ginger, the State says you did steal it, and they claim they've got the evidence to prove it. And they do. There's no question you took it from the picnic area and the police later found it at your apartment. No denying that."

Troubles and Kuddles

Tears filled Ginger's eyes. "Whatever evidence they have, Mr. Meek, it'll be totally false. I did not shoot at him, and I thought he left Kuddles there for me to take home, and that's the truth."

"But Ginger, if the jury does not believe you, I don't need to tell you that you're up the proverbial creek."

"This isn't fair, Mr. Meek."

Deloris ran a hand over his face and over the back of his neck. "Well, maybe not. But that's the way it is. Listen to me, Ginger, by accepting their offer, you will be able to avoid being sent to the penitentiary. If we go to trial, we'll be rolling the dice. And if we lose, you'll likely be sent off to prison for who knows how long, particularly if they convict you of the assault. The robbery charge alone carries twenty-five years."

Ginger, with tears running down her cheeks, said, "Mr. Meek, ever since you told me to expect an offer of a plea bargain, I've thought about what I'd do if they did it. I decided I couldn't be dishonest with myself. I will not live a lie, Mr. Meek, and that's what I'd be doing if I said I was guilty of something I didn't do. So, you can tell them I am pleading not guilty because I am not guilty. If I'm convicted, I'll have to live with that consequence. The Bible says everything happens for the best for those who love the Lord, and I believe that one hundred percent."

A silence followed.

"You're sure that's what you wanna do, Ginger? Turn down their offer?"

Ginger sighed as tears continued to flow. She nodded. "Yes, I'm sure," she said in a monotone voice. I will deal with whatever is my fate. There'd be a purpose for it. My faith tells me that."

"There's one other choice. You could plead *nolo contendere*."

"What's that?"

"It means 'no contest.' You don't admit or deny the charges. In effect, you'd be saying you don't contest the State's case."

"Sounds to me like a guilty plea, Mr. Meek," Ginger said, digging for a tissue in her purse.

"Yes, it is and it ain't, but in legal effect that's how the judge would treat it."

Deloris and Ginger sat in silence for a moment, with Deloris staring off at nothing in particular.

Deloris slapped his pants leg. "Okay, Ginger, I'll tell them we're gonna go to trial." He stood. "You know, of course, Ginger, the only thing we'll have to offer in your defense is your testimony. But like I have to tell you, your defense—at least regarding you running off with Kuddles—is undercut by the fact you did take her home with you."

"Yes, sir. But I didn't intend to steal her, Mr. Meek, that's the truth, so help me God." Ginger's body shook as she began to weep. "I just couldn't leave Kuddles out there at that place all by her lonesome."

***

Much to Deloris' surprise, Solicitor Virgil Parrish, a middle-age man of small statue and graying chestnut hair, decided to conduct the prosecution himself rather than allow one of his assistants to do it. After Parrish arraigned Ginger on an indictment alleging she had committed the offenses "against the form of the statute in such case made and provided and against the peace and dignity of the State," the two sides selected a petit jury consisting of six men and six women to decide the case. The Honorable Gerry Davis, the presiding judge, empaneled the jury and allowed the prosecution to make an opening statement, reserving the right of the defendant to offer one when it came time for her to present her case.

Parrish rose from his seat and paraded over to the petit jury box where he again published the indictment. He flubbed several words in the process, prompting Dixie, who sat behind Ginger and Deloris on the other side of the railing to lean forward and whisper in Deloris' ear, "I bet those three-syllable words will get him every time."

She proved a prophet. Parrish had particular trouble with the word "aforesaid," pronouncing it "AFF-oar-said" and "a-foe-REE-said" before correctly pronouncing it "a-FOUR-said."

Dixie leaned over the railing again to speak to Deloris in a whisper. "Is he as dumb as he sounds?"

Deloris ignored her. He did so because he did not know how smart and clever Parrish might be. Parrish and he had never met before, and all Deloris knew about Parrish's reputation as a trial lawyer was he could be rather feisty. Parrish had been solicitor long enough and re-elected often enough to avoid questions regarding his competence as a prosecutor.

After publication of the indictment, Parrish gave the jurors a brief opening statement in which he said the case would boil down to a swearing contest in which they would be asked to believe either a man ordained by God or a former nightclub performer now reduced to inspecting bottles at a soft-drink plant or, as he phrased it, "a person who looks for dirt among the washed."

Parrish called as his lead-off witness the person allegedly assaulted and the judicially declared owner of the ventriloquist dummy in question. As Parrish took his place at the farther end of the petit jury box, the clerk of court administered the oath to the witness.

Smiling broadly at the witness, Parrish launched into his direct examination. "Tell us your name, please sir?"

The witness smiled back. "My name?" His chest swelled. He sat up straight in the witness chair. "Mr. Solicitor, I am The Reverend Dr. James Holcomb, D.D.H."

"D.D.H.?"

"Yes, sir. Stands for Doctor of Divine Healing."

"Uh-huh, I see. So you're not a regular doctor?"

The question seemed to surprise Holcomb. He drew his chin back against his neck and made a face, his eyes widened. "Am I a regular doctor? I believe I'm as regular and as successful as any other doctor hereabouts, and I ain't never been sued for malpractice, like a lot of them have been, so I've been told."

"Where'd you get your doctorate? Which college?"

"Not no college. I give it to myself."

"Gave it to yourself?"

"Why sure. Why not? I'd done healed me I don't know how many folks all across this fair land of ours—people on crutches, in wheelchairs, in bed all the time, tongue-tied little boys, hard-of-hearing old folks—you know, the dumb and the deef. I've healed all kinds of sick people and them what was hurting from one thing or another. Back pain, lumbago, bad blood. You name it. Polio, piles, snake bite. Even healed a fella who'd been bitten by a bat.

"Look here, when you've healed as many folks as I have over the years, you don't need no what I call an 'edumication' or some highfalutin-looking paper what's been framed real nice to say you're a doctor when your experience has done made you one. Jesus didn't need no certificate from the Romans or the Sanhedrin to heal folks, and I don't need me no certificate from the State to heal them neither." He slapped his knee. "This might interest you. I even cured this man of rackets one time."

"Rackets? You mean 'rickets,' doncha?" Parrish offered.

"It's the same thing, only it's a whole lot worser case."

"How'd you do that?" Parrish asked.

Judge Davis interrupted the examination before Holcomb could answer. "Counsel, you best get on with the facts of this case. While some may find what the good reverend has to say interesting about his medical successes, we do, after all, have other cases to try after we get done with this one, sir. You should know that."

"Yes, sir."

"Ask him about the alleged assault and the alleged theft of the dummy, Mr. Solicitor."

"Yes, sir. That's what I was about to do, Your Honor. Thank you."

Parrish bowed toward the witness. "Dr. Holcomb, tell me this, did you have occasion to be on Highway 711, which the locals refer to as Belle's Highway."

"When?"

"On September 2, this year, which was a Wednesday."

"I did, yes, sir. Was there at this little picnic area right outside of Awenasa. Me and Kuddles, we—"

"Kuddles?"

"Yes, sir. Kuddles. That's the name of the ventriloquist dummy what that woman seated over there by that big lawyer stole

Troubles and Kuddles

from me the day after she saw fit to take a shot at me." Holcomb pointed to Ginger and scowled.

Deloris jumped to his feet. "Objection, Judge, Your Honor, sir."

"Overruled," said the judge. "Continue, Solicitor."

"But, Judge—"

"Did you hear me, Mr. Meek? I clearly said 'overruled.' I will say it again, sir. Overruled. Now, what did I say, sir?"

Deloris ducked his head. "You said, 'overruled.'"

The judge smiled. "Thank you, Mr. Meek. Continue Mr. Solicitor."

Parrish smiled at the jury. "What were you gonna say before Lawyer Meek saw fit to interrupt us? You and Kuddles, what were y'all doing there at this picnic site?"

"Having lunch. Least I was." Holcomb laughed. "Kuddles, she can't eat, you know, being she's a dummy—you know, a kinda big doll. She ain't real or nothing. Some folks believe she is, but she's not."

"Did you have Kuddles inside your car or outside with you?"

"I'd sat her across from me while I ate. I hate eating alone. She served the purpose, though she's not a real person—not a living, breathing one, she's not."

"Purpose?"

"You know, provided me some company."

"Did anything unusual happen while you were sitting there eating, you and uh—her?"

"No, huh-uh."

"How about later?"

"Uh-huh, later on."

"What?"

"Oh, well, I had to do something personal. So, I moseyed on down into the woods, leaving her there on the bench."

"What'd you have to do?"

Holcomb's face went pink for a few seconds. "I expected that question would be asked and I'd have to answer it without embarrassing everybody. So, I'll answer it thisaway. I had to do like *First Samuel*, Twenty-four, three, said ol' King Saul done when he went into that cave that time David and his men were hiding out in it. Little ol' David, he cut off part of Saul's clothes, and he done it without Saul even catching on that he done it," Holcomb said, snickering.

Parrish scratched the back of his head. "What's it say was the reason Saul went in there? I forget."

"It says he went in to cover his feet."

Parrish went blank. "Went into the cave to cover his feet?"

"Yes, sir. To cover his feet."

"You mean he didn't have any shoes on?"

"I'm only saying what the Bible says."

"So you went out into the woods to cover your feet?"

"In a manner of speaking. Yes, sir."

"You didn't have on any shoes?"

"Oh, yes, sir."

"I'm not following you, sir."

"Let me put it like this, sir, and I find this embarrassing to say." Holcomb's face went pink again. "I squatted down to—uh—you know . . ."

Parrish's face also assumed a pink hue. So did those of several jurors.

"I think I got it now," Parrish said. "What, if anything, happened while you were in the woods, as you say, 'covering your feet'?"

"That's when I heard this car come driving up. Two or three minutes later, I heard a gunshot and this bullet, it come whizzing by over my head. If I hadn't been covering my feet, it might've hit me smack between my eyes. Next thing was I heard this car door slam shut and the car make a sound like it was, you know, scratching off."

"What'd you do after that?"

"I waited there a few more minutes and snuck back to the picnic area. That's when I saw Kuddles wasn't there no more."

"Did you get a look at the person who fired the shot?"

"No, sir."

"How about the car? Get a look at it?"

"No, sir. Heard it, that's all."

"Was there someone who was supposed to have met you there at the picnic spot at that particular time?"

"Yes, sir."

Parrish whirled around and faced the jury with a smile. "Tell these fine ladies and gentlemen who it was you were supposed to have met then and there, sir."

"Who?" He nodded at Ginger. "That woman right yonder, the defendant."

"Why'd she want you to meet her out there?"

"I never figured that out. She somehow found out where I was. She called me there at the motel and asked for a meeting. She said she had a proposition what might interest me. So, me being a curious sorta person, I agreed to meet here there, even though me and her'd had our problems, our differences." He leaned forward in his chair and said in a low voice. "She sued me one time, you know."

"Say what now?" Parrish said as he faced the witness stand once more.

"She sued me one time," Holcomb said in a louder voice.

"Sued you, sir, a soldier in the service of the Almighty?"

"Yes, sir, but I've forgiven her for doing that, sir. Bible says forgive, and that's what I done."

"Well still, she sued you. Why on earth did she do that for?"

"What for? Cause she wanted to get her hands on Kuddles, that's how come. She claimed Kuddles was hers."

"She wanted Kuddles, did she? Hmmmmm."

"Yes, sir. Didn't do her suing me like she done, though, cause me and my lawyer, we won the case hands down. Even beat her when she took it all the way to the court of appeals. Sure did. Beat her like a rented mule, we did. That's right. Both courts said I was Kuddles' true owner and Miss Childree didn't have no right to her at all."

Parrish withdrew a paper from a file folder he lifted off his counsel table. He read it over as the ticking of the courtroom clock broke the silence within.

"Oh yeah, I meant to ask you," Parrish said at last, "what time was she supposed to meet you at the picnic area?"

"Dinner time. You know, noon. That's why I brung me a sandwich out there and stopped and bought me a Dr. Pepper. It was my eating time, you see."

Parrish extended his arm toward the jurors and shook his hand as he pointed to them. "Tell these nice folks, what time was it when you got shot at?"

"Well now, Mr. Solicitor, I wasn't exactly looking at my watch when all that was going on, but I reckon it was a little after twelve noon. I'd gotten there about fifteen minutes ahead of meeting time and I'd done ate my sandwich and drunk my drink—well, most of it. There was still a little bit of it left in the bottle."

Parrish returned to his counsel table. "Oh, one more thing. What value would you place on the dummy, on Kuddles?"

"She's priceless, Mr. Solicitor. Simply priceless."

"I know, but everything made by man's got some value. What would you say she'd be worth if you were to sell her on the open market? More'n a hundred dollars?"

Deloris stood. "Objection, Your Honor. He's asking a leading question, sir. Plus—"

The judge waved Deloris down. "Overruled."

Deloris dropped to his seat, feeling embarrassed.

Parrish gestured to the witness.

"More'n a hundred dollars? Oh, heavens yes. Much more," Holcomb said. "Like me and you, Mr. Solicitor, she's one of a kind." After a pause, he added. "She's also a child of God, though made by man."

Parrish bent forward and opened a large suit case at his feet. From it, he withdrew a large doll-like figure and carried it to the witness stand. "Recognize this, Dr. Holcomb?"

Holcomb reached into his inside coat pocket and retrieved a pair of glasses. "Hand her here, please sir, and let me take a gander."

Parrish gave him the doll. Holcomb appeared to study it front and back. "Yes, sir. This here is Kuddles, my dummy. I use her in my children's ministry. The kids, they get a big kick outta her. She tells them Bible stories—you know, about Samson and young David." He faced the jury and smiled. "And, of course, Jesus, especially the boy Jesus."

Several jurors smiled back at Holcomb.

Holcomb, still facing the jurors, continued his testimony. "Ladies and gentlemen, y'all might not believe this, but this precious little thing, she's led a lot of children to Christ, she has. He shook his head. "And to think, somebody'd set her mind to stealing Kuddles, a servant of the Lord. I'll tell you what might've happened. It just could be the Devil gotta hold of Miss Childree and made her do what she done. That ol' sly fox, he got tired of hearing Kuddles tell little children about Jesus, and he must've thought he'd could put a stop to her doing that by getting Miss Childree to steal her away from me."

Deloris jumped from his chair. "Objection, Your Honor. I ask that you strike from the record the witness' remarks about the devil and so forth."

"Sustained. The jury will disregard Reverend Holcomb's speculation about devil and possibly influencing the defendant's actions."

Notwithstanding the judge's comments in response to Deloris' objection, three jurors directed angry looks Ginger's way.

"Was your possession of Kuddles interrupted, sir?"

"That day at the picnic area, right off the highway there, it was. The same day that woman yonder tried her best to kill me."

Deloris stood to object. "Your Honor, now I want you to strike the witness' statement that—"

"Overruled, sir," the judge said in a tired voice. "And sit down."

Parrish took Kuddles from Holcomb. "Your Honor, we would like Kuddles here marked as State's Exhibit No. 1."

The judge edged closer to his bench. "Any objection, Mr. Meek?"

"I guess not," Deloris mumbled. He felt defeated and the trial still had a long way to go.

"You guess not?" the judge said, his voice raised. "Is that what you said? I don't want any guessing about the introduction of the dummy in evidence. Do you object or not, sir. Yes or no. Speak out."

"No, sir."

"Thank you, counsel. Now that wasn't so hard was it? Admitted without objection," said the judge, his face flushed.

Parrish handed Kuddles to the court reporter who affixed a label to Kuddles' right cheek before setting the dummy on the floor next to his stenograph. The red tag made it appear the dummy had sustained a face wound.

Parrish smiled at the witness. "No further questions, Your Honor."

"All right, sir. Cross-examine, Mr. Meek," the judge responded.

Deloris, with a legal pad in his hand with a page of handwritten, proposed questions he and Dixie formulated, rose from his chair and stepped toward the witness stand. He flipped over several pages of the legal pad. "Brother Holcomb, Dr. Holcomb, Reverend Holcomb? Which one do you want me to call you?" he said, his eyes directed toward his notes.

"It don't make no nevermind. Whichever one makes you happy."

"Believe I'll call you Dr. Holcomb, since that's your latest title. Say you gave that title to yourself, did you?"

"That's right, with the Lord's permission. Sure did. You got a problem with that, lawyer?"

Deloris noticed a woman on the back row of the jury box dip her head once and, with eyes ablaze, stare holes through him. Her manner unsettled him more than he already was because of the judge's treatment of him.

He pressed on, nevertheless. "Say the Lord approved of it, did He—your use of the title 'doctor'?"

"Let me put it to you like this here, Lawyer Meek. He ain't told me not to use it."

"Uh-huh."

Out of the corner of his eye Deloris saw the woman repeat her earlier action, only this time with her arms crossed on her chest.

Deloris returned to his counsel table and walked behind where Ginger sat. He touched her shoulder. "Now the day you say this thing happened, did you ever lay eyes on this lady here, Ginger Childree?"

"But see, she was supposed to be there right when it happened. Now ain't that some coincidence? Somebody shoots at me just about the time she's supposed to be there. And get this, when I come outta the woods there, Kuddles ain't there no more, and the police—now get this too—they later find Kuddles at her place. Now what was I supposed to think? She's—"

Deloris raised his hand. "Your Honor, I object. He's not responding to my question. I ask that—"

The judge shifted around in his chair. "Listen to me, Mr. Meek. You, sir, opened the door. Overruled. And by the way, he did respond to your question."

Holcomb did not wait for Deloris to continue. "To further answer your question about who it was who shot at me, Lawyer Meek, you know as well as I do she'd been trying like the devil to get Kuddles back from me, by hook or by crook. Why, you even helped her sue me once when y'all tried to get her back, didn't you? So, no I didn't see her the day I got shot at, but I ain't stupid, you know. I can put two and two together. My mama, she didn't raise no idiot."

"Your Honor—" Deloris whined.

"Continue, Mr. Meek," the judge said, circling his hand.

Deloris sighed. "Yes, sir. Can you describe the car the shots were fired from?"

"I didn't see no car. Like I said, heard it when it drove up, heard it when it sped off."

"And after that—"

"Like I done told you. I come outta the woods and seen Kuddles wasn't there no more. Somebody'd . . ." He tilted his head toward Ginger and pronounced his words in a slow, melodic voice. "Somebody'd took her."

"But you did not see Miss Childree take her."

"No, sir. But one thing I do know, Lawyer Meek, the police found Kuddles in Miss Childree's apartment and I'm smart enough to know that dummy ain't walked no ten or fifteen miles to get there on her own."

Every juror guffawed, causing Deloris' face to light up like a traffic signal turning red.

"You say Ginger called you and set up the meeting?" Deloris said, trying to recover.

"Right."

"You didn't call her?"

"Sure didn't."

"She arranged the meeting between the two of you, you say?"

"That's right."

"Now, where were you staying at when she called you?"

"At the Pines Motor Court right outside Awenasa."

"Hadn't you closed down your tent meetings and been gone for some time? That is, you'd pretty much disappeared?"

"Well, naw. I didn't exactly disappear. I kinda done like Jesus done that time. You know, when He went into the desert that time and stayed for forty days."

"But you had left the Awenasa area, hadn't you?"

"Uh-huh, but only for a little while. Any law say I gotta stay put in one place all the time? Yeah, I went away for a bit. I did it to follow Jesus' example. Went off by myself to reflect on things. Ain't you never done that? You know, gone off by yourself somewhere to iron things out in your mind? If you ain't never done that, you're the only one."

"And you come back to Awenasa?"

"Well, this ain't no ghost you looking at." Holcomb pinched himself and smiled. "I'd come back, I stayed, and I'm still here. Look at me." Holcomb turned his right profile toward Deloris and pointed to his cheek and then turned his left toward him.

"But you weren't gone for forty days, were you?"

"Don't know 'bout no forty days, but I stayed till the Lord told me to come back."

"Lord told you to come back?"

"He sure did."

"Who'd you tell you'd come back?"

"Ain't told nobody."

"Did you go by your tent when you got back?"

"No, huh-uh."

"By your trailer parked behind the tent? The Airstream."

"Huh-uh."

"It was still there, wasn't it?"

"Uh-huh."

"Rather than go by your trailer where you could've stayed for free, you decided to pay money to stay in a motel—the Pines Motor Court?"

"I figgered they'd done shut off my electricity, and I wasn't 'bout to stay there without no lights on or air conditioning."

"When did you check in there at the motel? And be careful of your answer, because I can easily check to see if you're telling the truth."

Parrish stood. "Objection, Your Honor. Counsel's badgering the witness."

"Sit down, Solicitor. He's not badgering. He's threatening. There is a difference." the judge said.

Parrish quickly complied with the judge's order, frowning and mumbling to himself.

Deloris continued. "Well, when did you check in there?"

"If I remember correctly, it was the day before me and her talked about meeting one another at the picnic ground."

"And you maintain and you're telling this jury that although you didn't tell nobody you were back in Awenasa and were staying there at the Pines Motor Court, Ginger Childree was the one who telephoned you?"

"That's right. She sure did."

"As far as you know, is she clairvoyant?"

"Clairvoyant? Her? No, she's a ventriloquist."

"How'd she know to call you at the motel?"

"I dunno. She's your client. Ask her."

"I'm asking you."

"And I ain't got no idea how she come by my telephone number." Holcomb laughed. "Maybe she had a vision. Reckon?"

Deloris glanced at his notes, turning several pages. "So, this is what we have here. You leave Awenasa for a while, you come back to Awenasa, you don't tell nobody you've come back, you don't go by your tent or trailer, you check into a motel, and out of the blue Miss Childree telephones you there the very next day. Have I got that right?"

Holcomb raised his right hand. "Let me clear something up for you, please sir. Lawyer Meek, as a man of God, I done swore on the King James version of the Holy Bible, the only true version, to tell the truth, the whole truth, and nothing but the truth so help me God, and that's what I'm doing." Holcomb looked at the judge. "I don't know how she learnt where I was staying at, Your Honor. Somebody must've seen me or something and went and told her. Could've been maybe somebody who worked there at the motel told her, I dunno. Y'all can ask her, but she sure done it all right and called me there. I ain't had no reason to call her. I mean, what would I call her for? She done sued me once about poor little ol' Kuddles. What would I wanna mess around with her for, meet with her? I learnt a long time ago you don't poke a stick at a snake. No, sir, I didn't want nothing more to do with her, and I'll tell you something else. I still don't. She ain't nothing but trouble with a capital T." Holcomb straightened his tie. "I mean, would you, Judge, Your Honor, fool with somebody who done sued you? I betcha wouldn't and wouldn't nobody else would either."

The judge raised his hand. "Leave me out of this, please sir."

"Yes, sir," Holcomb said. "I'm sorry. But what I'm getting at is I don't know of nobody who'd wanna have dealings with somebody who'd done sued them. Now, that don't mean I don't believe in forgiveness, but before folks are entitled to forgiveness, you know what? They gotta do something to earn it—in my book, they gotta. Least they gotta act like they're sorry, and she ain't done that."

"Didn't you telephone her at the bottling plant where she worked and asked her to meet you there at the picnic area to discuss y'all's problems?"

"No, sir, I ain't done that. If she told you I done that, you know what? She's done bore false witness against me. I've preached enough about sin to know that's Commandment number nine. Grab that *Bible* off the clerk's desk there and go to *Exodus*, chapter twenty, if you ain't never read it before, and read it. See if I ain't right. Tell you something else. I didn't know she even worked at no bottling plant."

"You deny you called her?"

Parrish slid back in his chair, causing it to screech. "Your Honor, he's already asked that question. Can't we please move on? You've told him not to badger the witness, but he won't pay attention to you, Judge. You need to sanction him, sir. You know, hold him in contempt. Jail for a spell. That'd learn him."

The judge rolled his chair forward. "Mr. Meek, you've asked him whether he called Miss Childree. He said he didn't. You've gotten your answer. Now either ask him something else or sit down. Am I clear? The solicitor has a point. The repeated asking of the same question constitutes badgering, especially where the answer is clear and entirely responsive to the question."

Deloris hung his head and mumbled. "Yes, sir."

The judge turned Parrish's way. "And Solicitor Parrish? I don't need you, sir, to tell me how to run my court. Got that? Do it again, and you will be the one held in contempt and, as you phrased it 'jailed for a spell.' "

"Yes, sir," he said, his voice atremble, his face and neck aflame.

Deloris turned to go back to his counsel table but stopped after taking two steps. He again faced Holcomb. "One more question, Your Holiness."

"Let's don't be cute, Mr. Meek," the judge warned, smiling.

"Yes, sir," Deloris said. "My question is this. When Ginger got to the picnic area and took custody of Kuddles, you'd already left there, hadn't you?"

"No. I was way back there in the woods. I done told you that," Holcomb replied.

"But that's just what you say, isn't it?"

"Huh?"

"Is there anybody else who could back up your story?"

Holcomb looked over at the jury and laughed. "Not nobody but Kuddles, and she ain't talking."

Several jurors laughed.

Deloris faced the jurors and nodded at them. "Well, maybe we can get her to do that. Whatcha think?"

Holcomb hunched his shoulders but did not answer the question.

"So, you say you were, to use your words, "way back there in the woods."

"That's right."

"So far back you could not see the picnic area, right?"

"I don't know what you are getting at."

"You couldn't see the person who shot at you because of the dense foliage and trees, I gather."

"Mr. Meek, haven't you plowed this field already?" the judge asked. "Oh, go ahead on."

Deloris bent toward the judge. "Thank you, Your Honor. What's your answer, Doctor?"

"Oh. Right. I couldn't see her."

"But you're telling this jury, aren't you, that despite the fact you could not see the person who you say shot at you because of all that vegetation, trees, and so forth, the person who shot at you could see you. Have I got that right?"

"Well, they shot at me, didn't they?"

"That's what you say happened." Deloris flipped a page of his yellow pad. "Let me ask you this. Did the police search for any bullets in the woods or find any spent shells in the picnic area?"

"I dunno."

"You don't?"

"They didn't tell me if they found anything. Ask them, why doncha?"

Deloris wheeled around and bowed to the judge. "Your Honor, I may not have any more questions, but if you will give me a second or two . . ."

Deloris walked back to his counsel table and went around behind it to confer with Dixie on the other side of the railing. "How about it? Anything else I should ask him about?" he whispered.

Dixie looked at him, her eyes opened wide and her head cocked to the side. "You mean you've forgotten all about Maxine Tumbleton? She's seated behind me, back there on the fourth row from the rear."

Deloris struck himself in the forehead with the heel of his palm. "Oh, stupid me. Thank you, Dixie. Man-o-man."

Dixie closed her eyes and shook her head, murmuring something Deloris could not make out.

Deloris returned to his former spot in front of the witness stand. "Your Honor, I do have a few more questions for this witness. I apologize for the delay."

"All right, counsel. Continue," the judge said in an even tone.

"Dr. Holcomb, you present yourself as a man of God, one of God's evangelists, right?"

Holcomb straightened his tie. "I not only present myself as such, I am as you say I am."

"I see. Are you married, sir?"

"Indeed, I am." Holcomb leaned to the side and looked out over the courtroom. "There she sits," he said pointing, "on the third row, right hand side, second from the left—the beautiful lady in the navy-blue suit and white blouse."

A plain-looking, thin, middle-age woman with long, graying hair stood with her head tilted to the side, a hand to her barren cheek. She offered her husband a weak smile.

Holcomb blew his wife a kiss and mouthed an "I love you" to her. A large silver cross hung from her long neck."

Deloris did not look the wife's way like most everyone else did. Some jurors stood and craned their necks as they looked for her in the courtroom.

"Are you, Dr. Holcomb, familiar with a woman named Maxine Tumbleton?"

"Who?"

"Maxine Tumbleton."

Holcomb scratched his head. "Tumbleton, Maxine Tumbleton, you say?"

"Yes, sir. You know her?"

Holcomb squirmed in his chair his head lowered. "Sir, I . . . I am trying to place her. Can you please give me a little more information about her?"

"She's a somewhat large woman, right pretty face, well-dressed. Worked for a magistrate here in Greenfield County. I believe you danced with her one night in your tent."

"I'm sorry, sir. I can't place her. I've danced with thousands in praise of Jesus, sir."

"Let me do this. Why don't I have her stand and let you look at her and see if that won't jog your memory. Okay?"

Deloris thought he saw Holcomb smile. "Will Maxine Tumbleton please stand," Deloris said as he faced the spectators.

The courtroom became quiet. Only the vehicular traffic outside could be heard. A humming sound arose when in the middle of the assembled on the left side of the courtroom a hefty woman in a gray jacket, a pale-yellow blouse, and a blue skirt stood and smiled toward Deloris. The drone wound its way through the courtroom but died away almost as quickly as it commenced.

"Are you Miss Tumbleton, ma'am?" Deloris asked.

"Yes, sir. I am."

Maxine waved to Holcomb. Holcomb smiled and waved back, laughing and winking at the jury as he did so.

Deloris motioned for Maxine to be seated. He faced Holcomb. "You recognize her, Doctor?"

"Can't say I do," Holcomb said.

"Can't say or won't?"

"Can't say."

"Did you get a good look at her? If not, I can have her stand again for you."

"That won't be necessary. I don't know her. Never seen her before in my life."

"You're absolutely sure now?"

"Yes. One-hundred per cent. If I remembered her, I'd tell you. I swore to tell the truth, Mr. Meek, and I've told you the truth."

"But, sir, I saw y'all waved to each other. What was that supposed to mean?"

Right away Deloris knew he had asked the wrong question because it afforded Holcomb an opportunity to offer an explanation for his action.

Holcomb crossed his legs, sat far back in his chair, and smiled at Deloris. "Correct me if I am wrong, Mr. Meek, but she waved at me first. I'm not in the habit of ignoring people who offer me a friendly greeting. Are you, sir? If somebody says 'good morning' to me, I'll say 'good morning' back. If someone waves at me, I'll wave back. Wouldn't most folks? Oh, and I'll tell you this, too. If somebody hugs me, I'll hug them back. And if somebody kisses me, I'll kiss them back. Well, let me amend my last statement. If the person who kisses me is a woman, I'll kiss them back." Holcomb laughed. "I ain't 'bout to kiss no men, although Paul does tell us in *Romans* 16:16 and again in *Second Corinthians* 13:12 to 'Greet one another with a holy kiss'." Holcomb leaned toward the jurors. "But between you and me, I kinda look on what he said do as more of a suggestion than an order, particularly when it comes to us men giving each other a smooch." He laughed again.

The jurors joined Holcomb in laughter.

Deloris ducked his head as he waited for the laughter to subside. Holcomb, meanwhile, rolled his tongue against his inside cheek, his eyes dancing.

Once the courtroom became quiet again, Deloris crossed his arms across his chest and said, "Sir, may I make this observation. If you told us a falsehood about not knowing the lady who stood a while ago, can we take it your testimony about what happened at the picnic ground is also a falsehood?"

"Objection, Your Honor. Counsel knows—"

"Sustained."

The judge's ruling did not upset Deloris. He had made the point he wanted to make, one he trusted would be brought home to the jurors when he later called Maxine to the witness stand.

Still, Deloris returned to his seat, unsure whether his cross-examination had gone well notwithstanding Holcomb's denial of his having previously known Maxine Tumbleton. As for his denial, Deloris thought it much too forceful and self-assured. This troubled him as did Holcomb's response to Deloris' remark about Holcomb's and Maxine's action of waving to each other. Passing it off as Holcomb did simply as a friendly greeting undercut any contention the act represented one of mutual recognition.

Deloris dropped onto his chair, his shoulders drooped and his hands between his thighs. He could not bring himself to look at Ginger. His case now, he determined, depended on Maxine Tumbleton, a person about whom he had grave misgivings.

Parrish next called the detective who found Kuddles in Ginger's apartment.

On cross-examination of the officer, Deloris asked two questions: whether a search of the picnic area had produced the bullet Holcomb claimed had whizzed by his head and whether he had discovered a gun when searching Ginger's apartment. To both questions, the detective answered "no."

After Deloris sat down, Parrish announced the State rested.

***

Following a brief recess, Deloris made a perfunctory motion for a directed verdict of acquittal. As Deloris expected, the judge deferred the motion, preferring to hold off on making a final ruling until all the evidence was in.

The judge, sitting erect, addressed Deloris. "All right, Mr. Meek, I understand the defendant will offer evidence in her defense. Your first witness please."

Deloris summoned Ginger to the witness stand where she took the required oath.

"You are Ginger Childree, the defendant in this case?" Deloris said as he stood between his counsel table and his chair.

"Yes, sir."

Deloris spent several minutes exploring her background before inquiring about her career as an entertainer and later as a tent evangelist in which she used Kuddles in a children's ministry.

"Why did you leave the ministry, Miss Childree?" Deloris asked.

Ginger shifted around in her chair. "Actually, Mr. Meek, I didn't leave the ministry. No, it left me."

Deloris bit his lip. "Hmmmm. Wanna explain that, please ma'am?"

"Okay. We had been several weeks in this place near Winston-Salem, North Carolina. Brother Holcomb came to my trailer one evening a few minutes before our nightly service was to begin and said—and these are his exact words—'We've done milked this cow long enough. Last night, the love offering had only sixteen dollars and forty-eight cents in it out of a crowd of about fifty-two people, not counting the young'uns.' He said he'd decided to cut the service pretty short by not having a children's sermon, cutting out some hymns, and preaching a short sermon. He also planned to have only a short altar call.

"He told me he wanted me to get my things packed because he'd be closing down and we'd be leaving the next morning early. He said he'd already instructed the crew to start taking down the tent after the service and getting everything all packed and ready to go before sunup even if it meant they had to work all night long. He went on to tell me we could leave at first light whether they were through or not.

"I asked him where we would be going to next, and he said he hadn't figured that out yet. He said he'd have to talk to the Lord about it, and he'd let me know what He said, hopefully the next morning."

"How did him telling you all this make you feel?"

"First off, I thought it odd he would decide we should leave without his knowing where we were headed. Of course, I was surprised. But on the other hand, something like that happened a couple of times before. That is, he'd suddenly announced we'd be moving on to some other town, usually one real far, far away and in a different state. Those times, however, he'd at least tell me the name of the town. But not this time, he didn't. That's what surprised me. He didn't have a town in mind."

"Would he always give a reason for moving on?"

"Once before when we—"

Parrish rose from his chair. "Your Honor, I don't see the relevance—"

The judge nodded and smiled. "Are you objecting, Mr. Solicitor?"

"Yes, sir, I sure am."

"Overruled. Continue, Mr. Meek."

"You were saying . . ."

"Once or twice before, when he suddenly announced we'd be moving, I asked him what the hurry was and, like when he decided to move from the Winston-Salem area, he said the contributions were insufficient and we needed to find greener pastures. He said little David didn't take his sheep to the same pasture every day and Jesus didn't hang around Jerusalem all the time either."

"I see," Deloris said as he moved from behind his table. "Do you know whether he left behind a number of unpaid bills those times he left towns in a big hurry?"

"Objection, Your Honor," Parrish yelled out. "Whether Dr. Holcomb paid a bill or not has nothing to do with this case. He's gone from chasing rabbits to chasing rainbows. This isn't a collection case, for crying out loud."

The judge leaned back in his chair. "I agree with you, sir. Sustained. Mr. Meek move on to the relevant issues involved here. We haven't got time to go chasing after things that have nothing to do with the case at hand."

Deloris swallowed hard. "But Judge, Your Honor," he whined, "believability lies at the heart of this case, and whether or not the prosecuting witness stiffed some poor merchant or supplier, why that goes to that very issue—you know, whether he's truly an honest man, somebody who could be trusted to do the right thing, such as pay his bills and such. I mean, anybody who would stiff a creditor would—"

The judge shook his head. "Mr. Meek, there could be many reasons other than dishonesty why a person might not pay a bill that's due. For instance, the quality of service or materials provided—any number of reasons. Failure of delivery, breach of contract, mistake."

"But Judge—."

Judge Davis raised his hand. "We are not going on wild-goose chases, Mr. Meek. That's my ruling. If you disagree with it, I'm sorry. I suggest you note it somewhere as a possible basis for an appeal from an adverse judgment and move on to something more to the point."

Deloris hung his head and sighed. "What occurred the next morning, Miss Childree?"

"Well, during the night I heard the tent men working and motors starting and the like. The noise they were making kinda lulled me to sleep. Anyway, when I got up the next morning and looked at my alarm clock, it said ten something. I couldn't believe it. I ran to the front door and looked out—I didn't even bother to put on a house coat—and the only thing left in the field we'd been occupying was the trailer I was sleeping in. Everybody had gone—disappeared. Poof! Just like that. I couldn't believe it. I'd been left high and dry, so to speak. I'd slept through the whole thing. Made me wonder if somebody might've slipped me something to, you know, knocked me out cold. I can't remember ever sleeping like I did that night."

"They left the trailer you slept in behind, did they?"

"It didn't belong to the y. He rented it locally. He often did that if somebody didn't donate one to the crusade, as the sometimes did. The people that owned mine came out a day or so later and got it. That's when I left and went to find you."

"How about your ventriloquist doll Kuddles?"

Ginger wiped her eyes with a flowered handkerchief she withdrew from her purse. "The last time I saw Kuddles, she was on the stage, propped up against her carrying case right behind the organ. The next morning, I looked around my trailer inside and out, but didn't see her. I next walked around the area where the tent and all had been and in the field behind there. I didn't see anything but the trash and garbage they'd left behind, and they left plenty of that, I'm telling you. I went through it all, looking for

Kuddles, but I never found her. I figured Brother Holcomb must've taken her."

"How'd you come by that conclusion?"

"How? About a month or so before we left North Carolina, he'd come to me and wanted me to teach him how to throw your voice—you know, how to be a ventriloquist. I asked him why, and he said he was just interested, that was all, that it looked like fun and besides, he said, he might have to substitute for me if I ever got sick. Stupid me, I agreed to teach him, helping how to use sound substitutions . . ."

"Young lady, did you say 'sound substitutions'?" the judge asked.

Ginger smiled at the judge. "Yes, sir. There are certain sounds you can't say without moving your lips. Sounds like those which begin with a 'p' or a 'v' and some others. You can say all of the vowels without moving your lips. But for those letters you can't say without doing it, what a ventriloquist will do is use a sound substitute for the troublesome letters or sounds."

The judge scratched his head. "I guess I catch on." He motioned to Deloris. "I'm sorry, Mr. Meek. Please continue."

"So, you tried to teach Dr. Holcomb ventriloquism?"

"Yes, I did. In doing that, I let him practice with Kuddles. The morning when I found out they'd gone and left me and I couldn't find Kuddles, I put two and two together. Of course, time and subsequent events proved me right. He had run off with her. Stole her from me."

"Objection, Your Honor."

"Sustained, Mr. Solicitor. The jury will disregard the witness' statement that the prosecuting witness stole the dummy."

Deloris retrieved his legal pad, flipped a few pages, and read one of its pages. "Let's jump ahead, Miss Childree. Mention has already been made to your suing Brother Holcomb in an attempt to recover your dummy."

"Yes, sir."

"And you lost the case, both before the trial judge and the appeals court, right?"

Ginger sniffed and nodded. "Yes, sir. Both courts."

Troubles and Kuddles

"As a consequence of having lost in your effort to regain possession of what you claimed was your ventriloquist dummy, what had you decided to do?"

"To have me another one made."

"Anything else?"

"Yes, sir. Me and my old partner, Wally Teal, happened to meet again, and we discussed forming a new act with brand new dummies and new material."

"In the meantime, what have you been doing to support yourself, Miss Childree?"

Ginger crossed her legs and pulled at the hem of her dress. "I've been inspecting bottles at a local bottling plant, making minimum wage." Ginger glared at the solicitor. "It's honest work, important work, and I'm thankful for the job."

"While you were there at the plant working, did you happen to receive a phone call on or about Tuesday, September 1, 1970?"

"Yes, sir. We had stopped the bottling process for our morning break. The phone rang in the break room, and I answered it. The lady in the office told me I had a call. She put the call through, and it turned out to be Brother Holcomb, of all people."

"What, if anything, did he say to you?"

"He said if I wanted Kuddles back, I could meet him the next day at the picnic area out on Belle's Highway about four or five miles out of town and we'd talk about how I could go about doing it. I told him I'd have to do it on my lunch break, and I'd have to borrow a car, but I didn't anticipate having any trouble borrowing one."

"So, I gather, you agreed to meet him there?"

"Yes, sir. We agreed to meet at twelve-fifteen. And the next day when I got my lunch break, I drove out there, arriving about twelve-thirty or so. I caught every red light in town, I do believe. I was a little late."

"Whose car did you borrow?"

"Oh, sorry. Mr. Calhoun's. He's the production manager. He lent me his. Nice man."

"What happened when you got there?"

"I pulled into the picnic area, parked the car. I didn't see anybody. For a moment, I thought he either hadn't gotten there yet or he had left since I didn't get there on time. That's when I saw Kuddles. She was sitting on one of the benches at a table."

"Did you see any other car?"

"No, I didn't. The one I was driving was the only one. All I saw was Kuddles."

"Kuddles? That's all?"

"Yes, sir. I figured Brother Holcomb must've left her there for me. I mean, why else would Kuddles be there and him not be? What would you've have thought, if you were me? Anyway, I waited a little while to see if he would return. When it looked like he wasn't going to, that's when I decided to take Kuddles back into town with me. If he hadn't meant for me to take her, he knew where I worked and could call me."

Ginger uncrossed her legs. "One thing I did, though before I put her in the car, I turned her every which way, looking for a note or something he might've left on her, but I didn't find one."

"I suppose you were surprised to find her there, were you not?"

"I sure was. What I figured was Brother Holcomb's conscience must've finally gotten to him, and he wanted to let me have her back."

Parrish stood. "Your Honor, sir, I must object and ask you to strike the witness' last answer from the record. She is obviously speculating, not offering facts, sir."

"Sustained. The jury will give no credence at all to what the witness says was the reason the ventriloquist dummy was there at the picnic ground. Put what she said completely out of your mind. Continue Mr. Meek."

"Yes, sir," Deloris said. He moved closer to the witness stand. "So, after you found Kuddles, what did you do?"

"I put her in the car and drove on back to the plant, happy as I could be. I couldn't wait to tell Wally. Having her back meant he and I might continue our routines with Kody and Kuddles. You know, as we did before."

"Kody?"

Troubles and Kuddles

"Yes, sir. That's Wally's dummy, the one that got damaged pretty bad one night in Louisiana in this nightclub we were playing at. Among other things, his head flew off when a heckler charged up onto the stage, grabbed hold of Kody, and used him to strike poor ol' Wally's head with it over and over." Ginger laughed. "What's funny is right when Mr. Meek there was headed up onto the stage to try and stop the man from killing Wally, that's when Kody's head came flying off. It hit Mr. Meek right here," Ginger said, pointing to her forehead. "The blow knocked Mr. Meek clean down the steps onto the floor." She laughed again. "You remember all that, don't you, Mr. Meek?"

Deloris rubbed his forehead while feigning a laugh. "Yes, I do. But I recovered in due course."

"Kody did too," Ginger said. "Wally got him repaired. He's as good as new now."

"Going back to what happened when you went out to the picnic area, do you own a gun, Miss Childree?"

"No, sir."

"Do you have possession of a gun?"

"No, sir. I have never in my life ever even fired one. For that matter, I've never even held one in my hand—not a real one, I haven't."

"Did you shoot at Brother Holcomb while at the picnic area on Highway 711 on September 2, 1970?"

"No, sir. I most assuredly did not."

"But you did take Kuddles away from there, did you not?"

"Yes, sir. Like I indicated a while ago, I thought he wanted me to. I thought he'd left her there for me to take home. I mean, why else would he call me and ask to meet him, and him not be there and leave Kuddles where anybody who'd stopped at the picnic area could've taken her? Frankly, I'm surprised nobody'd done that before I got there, if you wanna know the truth. Course, I don't know how long he'd been gone from the picnic ground."

Deloris moved behind his counsel table. He beaconed to Dixie to join him at the railing. He whispered to her. She shook her head.

"Your Honor," Deloris said, "that's all the questions we've got right now for Miss Childree."

Judge Davis scratched at his nose. "All right, sir. Cross-examine, Mr. Solicitor."

Parrish stood to question Ginger. "I suppose," he said, chuckling, "there wasn't anyone in the picnic area who could corroborate your story, is there?"

"I didn't see anyone, no sir."

Parrish glanced at the jury and winked. "Excuse me. I almost forgot. 'Miss What's Her Name'—the dummy . . ."

"Kuddles, you mean?"

"Miss Kuddles, she was there, wasn't she?" He laughed. "Excuse me, I had a funny thought. I wonder if even she would substantiate your story."

The judge interrupted. "Is that a question, Solicitor?"

Ginger looked at the judge. "Your Honor, excuse me. I took that to be one. If I may, I'd like to answer it, please sir."

The judge drew back and stared at Parrish. "What say you, Solicitor?"

Parrish glanced around at the jury, grinning. "Tell you what. Let her talk, if she can," he said with a laugh.

Most all the jurors laughed as well, one juror slapping his thigh and whispering something to the juror on his right, who doubled up in laughter.

Ginger did not wait for the judge to react to Parrish's remark. "My answer to his question is yes, she would support my testimony." She smiled at the court reporter. "If you'd hand Kuddles to me, please sir, I'll show you."

The reporter appeared confused. "Hand her?"

Ginger smiled and pointed. "Kuddles, the little lady there on the floor. You know, State's Exhibit No. 1."

"Oh, right!" the reported said. He handed the puppet to Ginger.

She set Kuddles in her lap and inserted her hand into a slit in its back. A second or two later Kuddles' head turned.

Parrish stood watching, his eyes first directed toward the witness stand and then toward the jury. He appeared thoroughly amused. He took a step toward Ginger and motioned for her to stop. "Excuse me, Miss Childree, could I have your attention for a moment? I'd like for you to quit playing with the pretty little dolly, if you don't mind, please ma'am, and allow me to continue. I'm about through."

Ginger blushed. "I'm sorry. I was checking her out. I wanted to make sure she was in working order before I let her talk."

"To let her talk?"

"I had understood you wanted me to ask her about what happened when I went to the picnic area and took her away from there that day. Am I right, sir?" Ginger asked with a smile.

Parrish grunted. "Well, that's not at all necessary. There are other matters we need to discuss right now. I'm afraid we won't have time for a floor show."

Deloris noticed some jurors frowning. He sensed their disappointment in not seeing Kuddles perform.

"Excuse me, if Your Honor please," Deloris said, standing. "I also thought the solicitor wanted Kuddles to testify about what had happened out there in the roadside park. Did I misunderstand?"

The judge nodded. "Yes, sir, Mr. Meek. That was my impression also."

Parrish wrung his hands. "But . . . but, Your Honor, surely you didn't take what I said seriously." He chuckled. "You didn't honestly think I wanted to allow a ventriloquist dummy to testify. Obviously, I was being facetious. Your Honor must know that, sir." He turned to the jury with his arms extended and his hands opened.

"No, sir, I don't know that," the judge said, using an annoyed tone. "You, of all people, Mr. Solicitor, as many cases as we've been involved in together, should know, when I am presiding over a case, I want to be able to take lawyers at their word. If you don't mean what you tell me in open court and on the record, Solicitor Parrish, you ought not to say it at all. Courts cannot operate efficiently if a lawyer can tell a judge one thing and later, when the court relies on what the lawyer says, the lawyer can claim he didn't mean what he had earlier said. In my discretion, I will permit the witness to testify through the dummy. After all, sir, you are the one who opened the door to this form of testimony." The judge smiled at Ginger. "We're all waiting to hear from Miss Kuddles, ma'am."

Ginger adjusted Kuddles, turning the dummy toward the jurors.

Before Ginger could speak, Parrish interrupted. "Your Honor, aren't you going to swear the witness?"

The judge whipped his head around and glared at Parrish. "What's that you say, sir?"

Parrish's face reddened. "I was merely inquiring whether the clerk should administer an oath to the dummy since, in your discretion, you will permit it to testify."

The judge's mouth dropped open. "Is this an attempt to be funny, Mr. Solicitor, or have you suffered a complete loss of your senses? Don't you know a ventriloquist dummy itself cannot speak, that what words which appear to come from a dummy's mouth are those of the operator, in this case Miss Childree? And if memory serves—and I believe the record will so reflect—Miss Childree has been sworn as a witness."

"Yes, sir, Your Honor," Parrish said in muffled voice. "Very good."

The judge addressed Ginger. "You remember taking the oath, do you not, Miss Childree?"

"Oh, yes, Your Honor," Ginger said.

"You may proceed."

Ginger had Kuddles dip its head and smiled at the jury. Several of the jurors, smiling, scooted forward in their chairs as Ginger got her examination underway. One juror held a hand to his ear.

"Kuddles, honey," Ginger said, "how long have we known each other?"

"Since you got me created by that nice man several years ago," Kuddles appeared to say.

"You remember Kody and Wally Teal?"

"Sure do, but I didn't like Wally. I liked Kody. He was kinda cute. My type, if you catch my drift." Kuddles' eyebrows raised and lowered several times.

Some jurors laughed as did several of the spectators.

"Do you remember when you and I joined Reverend Holcomb's crusade and you became a child evangelist?"

"Got saved, you mean?"

"Yes."

"I remember."

"After that, didn't you preach to the children who would come to our revival services?"

"Well, me and you would do that."

"And did we stop one day from doing that?"

Kuddles' head tilted downward. "Yes."

"Why, if you know?"

"I don't know why it happened, but early one morning Brother Holcomb got me, put me in my carrying case, and we left you behind near some place in North Carolina with a strange name."

"A strange name?"

"Yeah. They called it 'Wish I Could Go Sailing.'"

The court room erupted in laughter.

Ginger joined in. "No, darling, it's called 'Winston-Salem,' not 'Wish I Could Go Sailing.'" She rearranged Kuddles on her lap. "Do you remember when I finally caught up with you and the preacher and I tried to get you back?"

"Yes, but the court wouldn't allow it. They said I belonged to the preacher. He said you'd given me to him."

"Did I do that?"

The solicitor objected. The judge sustained his objection and instructed Ginger to restrict her questions to the matter at hand, namely the criminal charges.

Ginger nodded and resumed her testimony. "Do you remember going to a picnic area not too long ago?"

"Yes. He took me there, Brother Holcomb did. He set me on a bench by one of the tables. After he did that, he got in his car and drove off, leaving me out there all by myself. After a few minutes, you came and got me and took me to your place. Later on, the police, they came and took me with them to the police station."

"While I was at the picnic ground, did you see me shoot at Brother Holcomb?"

"Nome."

"Did you hear any kind of gunshot while I was there?"

"Nome."

"Did you see me with any kind of a weapon at all in my hand?"

"Nome."

"When he left you there on the picnic bench, what did you think was happening?"

Parrish raised his hand. "Now, Your Honor, a ventriloquist dummy can think? I—"

"Sustained. Go on to something else, Miss Childree."

Ginger removed her hand from Kuddles' back. "I'm through, Your Honor."

The judge rocked back and forth a couple of times in his chair. "All right, Mr. Solicitor, you may question the witness, if you please. That, of course, includes the dummy."

"Thank you, Your Honor, you are most gracious," Parrish said smiling as he stood behind his table. He slipped sideways and walked toward the witness stand.

"Miss Childree, just so we are all clear about this, the show you put on for us a moment ago, you did all the talking, right?"

Ginger's eyes widened. "Why certainly."

Parrish turned and winked at the jury. "By the way, I saw your lips move."

"I'm a little out of practice."

"Let me clarify something, if I may. Your words were your words and Kuddles' words were your words, right?"

"Yes, sir. I thought everybody—"

"So, Kuddles says whatever you want her to say, right?"

"When I'm operating her, yes, sir."

"I'm just asking you these basic questions just for the record. In short, you deny shooting at Dr. Holcomb but admit taking Kuddles from the picnic area, correct?"

"Yes, sir."

"Did Dr. Holcomb give you express permission to take Kuddles?"

"Not express permission."

"Was that the Christian thing to do, Miss Childree? Taking her without express permission?"

"Under the circumstances, yes, sir."

"Was it indeed? Well, let's see about that. Wasn't one of those circumstances he had fought you tooth and nail all the way to the court of appeals of this state, right?"

Rather than answer, Ginger re-inserted her hand into Kuddles back. "Boy, am I glad she got me away from that picnic area. I saw this big ol' woodpecker . . ." Kuddles appeared to say.

Parrish seemed startled. "Now Your Honor, this witness is attempting to turn this into a vaudeville act. I object."

The judge shook his head. "Don't do something like that again, Miss Childree. Okay?"

Ginger nodded and responded in a small voice. "Yes, sir."

Parrish continued. "In your battle over ownership of State's Exhibit No. 1, the courts, they have all ruled Kuddles belongs to Dr. Holcomb and not you, have they not?"

"Yes."

"And you have had an extremely difficult time accepting their judgment too, haven't you, Miss Childree?"

"That's because they got it all wrong."

"Oh, they did, did they?"

"Yes, sir. They did."

"And the 'they' includes the judges on the court of appeals panel, right?"

"Yes, sir."

"All three of them?"

"Yes."

Parrish glanced at the judge. "So the judges, these honorable, learned men, according to you now, they have condoned an act of stealing—the theft by a man of the cloth, a man of God—of a ventriloquist dummy? That's pretty much what you claim they all have done, am I right?"

"All I'm saying, sir, is they got it wrong. Judges are not infallible."

"The heck you say. Well, let's count the judges you say got it wrong. There's the trial judge. That's one." Parrish faced the jury and raised the index finger of his right hand. "And there are the three members of the appellate court." Using his left hand, he displayed three of its fingers and displayed them to the jury along with the one finger on the other hand. "That's four judges altogether. And you say they were all wrong? All four were, shall I say, 'fallible.' "

Ginger twisted around in her chair and pulled at her skirt. "Yes, sir, in my opinion."

Turning toward Ginger again, he asked, "And exactly what training have you had as a lawyer or as a jurist, ma'am?"

"None."

"I didn't suppose you had, ma'am. Not for one moment."

"Truth is not determined by numbers, Mr. Solicitor."

"Really? Are you sure about that? But we wander." Parrish stood fully erect with his hands to his hips. "Again, ma'am, you assumed Dr. Holcomb wanted to give you back the dummy after he'd already spent a whole lot of money on the best lawyers he could find in an attempt to keep you from getting it back. Am I right?"

Ginger did not answer.

Parrish faced the jury. "Money, ma'am, he could've better spent doing the Lord's work instead of spending it on the lawyer fees and court costs necessitated by the meritless lawsuit you and Mr. Meek saw fit to bring—a law suit over, of all things, a little ol' dummy."

A quiet enveloped the courtroom.

"And ma'am to top it all off, after four judges ruled against your position, didn't your lawyer tell you that you could try to get the five members of the state supreme court to review your case?"

"I don't remember, sir."

"Did you seek further review of your case by the state supreme court, Miss Childree?"

"I guess not."

"I take that as a no, ma'am. One other question and I'm through. "What made you assume he hadn't ridden someplace to buy him a cocola or use a phone or something and would've driven back in a few minutes."

"But I waited for a few minutes. I honestly did."

"Oh, I bet you did," he said, sneering. He pulled at the waist of his trousers and smirked. "Thank you, ma'am." He bowed to the court. "That's all my questions, if Your Honor please."

The judge folded his arms and rested them on his desk. "All right. Let's have your next witness, Mr. Meek."

"Please give me a moment, sir."

"Yes, sir."

Deloris used the opportunity to confer with Dixie about his next move. "I know we have subpoenaed the Tumbleton woman," he whispered, "but do I really wanna call her as a witness. I can't explain it, but I don't have a good feeling about putting her on the stand. Whatcha think?"

Dixie blew some hair out of her face. "You know, Deloris, I expressed misgivings about that woman once before, if you remember." Dixie rubbed the back of her neck. "But the way I see it now, you don't have any choice but to put her up. That's because you made such a big deal about whether Holcomb knew her or not." She crossed her arms. "Anyway, that's my opinion. You wanted it, and now you've got it."

Deloris thought a moment about what Dixie said. He made a decision that troubled him to make. "If Your Honor please, the defense calls Maxine Tumbleton."

"Come around and be sworn, ma'am," the judge said.

As Maxine came forward, a backwash of cheap perfume followed her to the witness stand. When administering the oath, the clerk of court kept one hand under the Bible, one hand to his nose, and his head turned away from the witness. The judge, apparently catching a whiff of her smell, rolled his chair away from the witness stand to the farther side of the bench.

Deloris remained a safe distance away, electing to stand behind his counsel table. He first delved into Maxine's background, principally her employment with the court system.

"Now, Miss Tumbleton, take a good look at the prosecuting witness and tell the court whether you have ever seen this man before today?"

She smiled. "Oh, yes, sir."

"Yes, sir, what?"

"I've seen him before. I saw him one night at a revival service."

"Tell us about that, please ma'am."

She hunched her shoulders. "Not much to tell. One night me and a friend, we went to his revival tent—out of curiosity mainly. He preached a sermon. That's when I saw him."

"And what happened after that, ma'am?"

"What happened after that? Me and my friend, we left there and went to Ro-Lo-Jac's down the road and bought us banana split. After I dropped her off at her place, I went on home and went to bed because I had to rise and shine kinda early and go to work the next morning at the courthouse."

Maxine's answer stunned Deloris, but he continued on without showing it had that effect. "I see. Did you answer an altar call when you were at the revival that night?"

"Who me? No sir."

Didn't you go down front and he laid his hands on you, ma'am?

"Sure didn't. I'm already saved."

"But you later returned, didn't you, I mean you maybe went another night to a service?"

"No, sir. I never did go back. I only went that one time."

Deloris swallowed hard. "Say what now?"

"I never went back there. I never saw Mr. Holcomb again after that night when me and my friend went there and later on we got us some ice cream. Well, not until today, I hadn't seen him."

Deloris spun around and looked at Dixie and Ginger. Each sat with her eyes and mouth agape.

He confronted Maxine again. "During the service, didn't you go down front and get up on the stage and dance with Brother Holcomb, Miss Tumbleton?"

She laughed. "You asking me if I danced with Dr. Holcomb?"

"Yes, ma'am, while the organist was playing 'Jesus on the Telephone,' or something like that?"

"I believe you've got me confused with somebody else. I don't dance, and certainly not in church. My mama taught me it was a sin to dance."

"So, you deny you danced with Dr. Holcomb during one of his revival meetings, Miss Tumbleton?"

"Yes."

"Miss Tumbleton," Deloris said, his voice shaking and a finger pointed at Ginger and Dixie, "didn't you have lunch with me and my client and my secretary, those two ladies who are seated right over there, and tell us you answered an altar call given by Brother Holcomb and before that you and him—"

"Your Honor," Parrish said, standing, "excuse me, counsel, but I've been patient, but I must object. Counsel is attempting to impeach his own witness, a highly improper move, Your Honor. I'm surprised he doesn't know any better."

Judge Davis sighed. "Mr. Meek, sir, you cannot do that. You called this lady as your witness and by doing it you vouch for her. I cannot, without more, allow you to cross-examine her."

"But Judge, she's—"

"I agree with the solicitor. You should know you cannot impeach your own witness, sir. Now, follow the rules, Mr. Meek. Do you have any more questions—any more proper questions you wish to ask this witness, sir?"

So caught up in a moment he had not anticipated, Deloris could not think straight. He could not remember how to remedy the situation by having the court declare the witness a hostile witness and thereby allow him to cross-examine her. He stood mute, sensing Ginger's defense crumble. He spun around and motioned to Dixie who met him at the railing.

Deloris wrung his hands. "Dixie, I don't know what to do. Can you think of anything."

Dixie shook her head. I'm sorry, Deloris. I don't. Does this means you can't use me or Ginger to tell about what she told us at the café?"

"I believe so. I'm scared to even try to do that, now." He inhaled. "Durn it all, I wish I could call Billy Joe."

"Oh, pshaw," Dixie said, "he wouldn't know what to do either. You give that man far too much credit."

"Train time," Mr. Meek," the judge called out. "Train time."

Deloris hung his head and turned to face the judge. "Yes, sir. Your Honor. I don't have any further questions of the witness."

"Miss Tumbleton," the judge said, pointing to the floor, "you can step down, ma'am. I assume, Mr. Solicitor, you don't have any cross-examination, do you, sir?"

Parrish hesitated before responding to the court's inquiry. He halfway stood. "Uh, I don't reckon so, Your Honor."

"I gathered that," the judge said, looking pleased with himself.

Judge Davis squinted at Deloris. "Any other witnesses, Mr. Meek?"

Deloris shook his head. No, sir. That's our defense, sir.

"That being the case, Mr. Solicitor, is there any reply?"

"Yes, sir. I recall Dr. Holcomb."

"Okay," the judge said, "come around sir. You are still under oath."

Holcomb hurried to the witness stand. Once seated, he turned and smiled at the jurors. Several smiled back at him.

"I've a few questions, Doctor." Parrish picked up Kuddles and handed the puppet to Holcomb. "And if you don't mind, Doctor, I have a few questions for Kuddles," he said still smiling.

Deloris pushed back in his chair. "Your Honor, I object. We've already had testimony from Kuddles. I mean, who's putting on a show now? I don't see—"

"Overruled. Sit down."

"Thank you, Your Honor," Parrish said. "Dr. Holcomb, briefly, I don't want to plow the same ground that we did in your earlier testimony, but there are a couple of questions I'd like to ask Kuddles. Do you know how to operate the puppet?"

"Yes, sir, with the Lord's help."

"Now, now, Reverend Holcomb," the judge said. "Let's leave the Lord out of it."

"Oh, I could never do that, if Your Honor please. That's what's wrong with the world today. Too many people are leaving the Lord out of it."

A chorus of "amens" filled the courtroom, prompting the judge to call for order.

Parrish walked to the far end of the jury box. "Dr. Holcomb, you placed Kuddles on a bench by one of the picnic tables, did you not?"

"Yes, sir."

"And that was before you headed for the woods for—shall I say?—a private purpose."

Holcomb nodded.

"Now this question is for Kuddles. Kuddles?"

Kuddles' head turned toward Parrish.

"Did you see Ginger Childree drive into the picnic area?"

"Yes," Kuddles appeared to answer but using a distinctive male voice.

"Did you see her put you into her car?"

Kuddles appeared to give another yes answer.

"One last question. Did you see Miss Childree shoot at Dr. Holcomb?"

"Yes, I did."

Parrish bowed toward the witness stand, "Thank you, Doctor, and thank you too young lady. You may cross-examine, Mr. Meek."

Before Deloris could stand, the judge announced a fifteen-minute recess. The recess could not have come at a better time because he now had no idea how best to go forward. He had not yet recovered from the Tumbleton debacle.

As the courtroom emptied of onlookers and court personnel, Ginger sidled next to Deloris as he stood in front of his counsel table much in thought. "Mr. Meek, sir, if you have a minute, could I have a word with you?"

Deloris, in no mood to be bothered, met Ginger's request with a sharp response. "I'm sorry, Ginger, not now please."

Ginger insisted. "This won't take but a minute." She handed Deloris a New Testament Bible into which a bookmark had been inserted. "I've got an idea about how you might can cross-examine Brother Holcomb. But first read the scripture I've got bookmarked there."

"Look, Ginger—"

"Please read it, and I'll explain how this might help us."

Deloris sighed. He opened the bible to the place bookmarked, *Luke* 8:28-38. He read it hurriedly. "Okay, I've read it, but I don't quite understand how I might could use it."

"This is how," Ginger said. She went on to explain.

***

The judge returned to the courtroom, and Holcomb retook his seat on the witness stand. As before, Kuddles sat in his lap. Once the courtroom quieted, Judge Davis motioned to Deloris. "All right, Mr. Meek, you may cross-examine, if you please."

Deloris came from around his table and stood, facing the jurors, about halfway between the witness stand and the far end of the jury box. "If you don't mind, Reverend, I've got a few questions for Kuddles, okay?"

Parrish was on his feet. "Now, Judge. This is getting a bit—"

"Sit down," the judge ordered. "Continue, Mr. Meek."

"Kuddles, you say you saw Ginger when she arrived there at the roadside park?"

With Holcomb providing Kuddles' voice, the dummy appeared to say, "Yeah."

"Are you male or female, Kuddles?"

The audience laughed.

Kuddle's head bent toward her ample chest. "I'm a girl, last time I looked. What, you can't tell?"

Troubles and Kuddles

"Well, you do look like a girl to me, but your voice, it's kinda got a funny sound to it. Is there something wrong with your voice? You're not hoarse or sick or anything, are you?"

"No," came the answer after some hesitation

Deloris smiled at the jury. "Maybe it's just me, but your voice strikes me as being on the deep side. You know, like a man's. Doesn't it sound male-like to you?"

Deloris got no answer.

"Let me ask you this. What was the name of your creator—the person who made you—put you together?" Deloris asked.

"I can't remember."

"You can't remember, or you don't know?"

"Don't know."

Deloris nodded and smiled. "I know it is impolite to ask a lady her age, but do you mind telling this jury how old you are?"

"I don't feel like answering your question."

The judge stared at Kuddles. "Answer it."

"Okay, I will. I don't know," came the response.

"Is the voice you are now using the one you've always used?"

"Yes. I mean, no it's not."

"You used to have a distinct female voice, didn't you?"

"A stinking female voice?"

"A distinct female voice."

"I don't know what that is?"

"I believe you do."

"A person's voice can change, you know."

Deloris rubbed the back of his neck. "I knew male voices changed, but I didn't think those of little girls did. Of course, I might be wrong."

"Wouldn't be the first time, I bet."

Deloris, his tongue to his upper lip, nodded. "Tell me, what brought about your voice change? Did your age have anything to do with it?"

"Could've, I reckon."

"But you don't know how old you are, do you?"

"No. I told you already."

"Isn't the reason your voice changed—and so quickly too—is because some other person or entity took over your body after Miss Childree held you in her lap?"

"You could say that."

"Your voice change had nothing to do with age, did it?"

"I guess not."

"Once before you spoke like a female, but you don't speak like that anymore and that's because somebody or something else assumed control over you, did they not? Kinda like demon possession, huh?"

"Objection, Judge. Inflammatory."

"Sustained."

"You familiar with Legion?"

"You mean the American Legion? Yeah."

"No, I refer to the demons Luke talks about in his gospel there in chapter eight, verse thirty."

"No."

"You're not? But your operator is a Christian evangelist, isn't he?"

"Yes, he is. Well, we both are. He's one, and I'm one. I do the kids."

"But aren't you and he one and the same?"

"We are but we ain't."

"Who are you when you're not the Reverend Dr. Holcomb?"

"Just me."

"You're a person called Just Me. And could Just Me be the same being the Bible calls 'Legion'?"

"No."

"You sure about that? Legion was a collection of beings who had entered a man, correct?"

"That's what you say the Bible says."

"Shall I read from chapter eight, verse thirty?"

"No. I'll take your word for it."

"Good. So, you will agree, will you not, that Legion—this collection of demons—represented an entity which was quite different from the man's original self?"

"I guess so, yes."

"And again, Legion was a collection of demons, right?"

"I suppose."

"And demons lie, do they not?"

"Objection, Your Honor," Parrish yelled from a seated position.

"Overruled," said the judge.

"You've told two different stories on this witness stand today, have you not?"

"No, I haven't."

Deloris' eyes widened. "You haven't, Kuddles? A while ago, you testified you saw Miss Childree shoot at Reverend Holcomb, but earlier you testified you did not see her do that. Aren't those two different stories? Well, aren't they?"

"She was lying."

"Who was lying?"

"Her."

"But the person you refer to as 'her' was actually you, Kuddles. Right?"

No response came.

"And when you told us Ginger did not shoot at Brother Holcomb, that was your original female self speaking, right?"

"Yes."

"The self that existed before another being took you over, right?"

Again, no answer came.

"That's all I have, Your Honor," Deloris announced.

The judge gestured toward Parrish. "Any redirect, Mr. Solicitor?"

Parrish shook his head. "I'm afraid I'd only muddy the water some more, Your Honor."

"I take that as a 'no.' Gentlemen, prepare for argument. We'll take ten minutes. Court will stand at ease."

***

When court reconvened, both lawyers argued their respective positions to the jury. The State elected to waive opening argument.

For his part, Deloris pounded away at the burden of proof required to convict Ginger—a verdict of guilty mandated her guilt be established beyond a reasonable doubt. He also harped upon the issue of credibility, pointing to the story of Legion recounted in the *Gospel of Luke*. As he did in his cross-examination of Holcomb, Deloris equated Holcomb's takeover of Kuddles' body with the demons' takeover of the man Luke wrote about.

Deloris ended his summation, delivered in a down-home fashion, by asking the jurors a question and answering it for them: "If somebody really did fire a gun at Brother Holcomb, Reverend Holcomb, Doctor Holcomb, Pastor Holcomb, Mister Holcomb, whatever title he goes by, when he was out there squatting in the woods with his britches down around his ankles, then how come he ain't shown us no bullet? I'll tell you how come. It's because, just like his name kinda sounds, his story is nothing but just a bunch of hokum. Gentlemen, there wasn't no bullet to show you, that's why the State ain't showed you one."

As for Solicitor Parrish, he recognized the case amounted to nothing more than a swearing contest and urged the jurors to believe the State's witness. "Who had the most to gain here?" he asked. "Not Dr. Holcomb. He already had possession and ownership of Kuddles.

"Moreover, he had ended his relationship with the defendant. She, on the other hand, had fought him like a tiger to regain possession of the dummy, and she'd lost at every turn. Her finding the puppet alone that day afforded her one last chance to get it back, no questions asked.

"Speaking of chances, it was only by chance Dr. Holcomb wasn't killed that day. The good Lord was with his servant that day. Dr. Holcomb may have lost his beloved puppet, but he didn't lose his life. Thank God, that woman's shot missed its mark—and believe me there was a shot, only we couldn't find it, the woods being the way they are. Had she hit him, we'd been trying a murder case today, gentlemen. Y'all give some thought to that, why don't you."

Parrish ended his argument with a reference to Maxine Tumbleton. "Talk about missing a shot, what was my good friend trying to pull here by putting Miss Tumbleton on the witness stand? Answer me that. He first asked the good reverend if he recognized her, and he said no, he didn't. Did that satisfy Mr. Meek. No, sir. Not one bit. What'd he do? He went and put the poor woman—who, by the way, is a court attaché—that's a court employee, in case you don't know French—put her on the witness stand and tried to get her to lie, that's what—"

Deloris jumped from his chair. "Your Honor, I object to counsel's attacking—"

"Sit down, Mr. Meek. This is jury argument."

Parrish chuckled. "Now where were we when we got so rudely interrupted? Oh, yeah. I remember. We were talking about Miss Tumbleton. What did Mr. Meek do? He asked Miss Tumbleton, whose daily work—her life—is devoted to the pursuit of truth and justice, whether or not she knew Brother Holcomb. You saw her. You heard her. She didn't know what in the heck he was talking about, did she? Now I want you to ask yourself a question, and if you answer it correctly, that answer will point you to what your verdict ought to be. My question is this: which side, the State or the defendant, attempted to pull the wool over your eyes? Was it us, or was it them right over there," he said with a finger pointed at Deloris.

At that moment, Deloris wanted to crawl under the table.

"I'm just about through, ladies and gentlemen. But before I sit down and let the judge tell y'all what the law is and how y'all are to go about deciding what verdict to return, I wanna say something about the burden of proof. Yes, my friend Mr. Meek was right when he told y'all before a guilty verdict can be returned in this case y'all've gotta find the evidence shows the defendant committed any one of these offenses beyond a reasonable doubt." Parrish drew close to the jurors and dropped his voice. "Let me tell y'all something. The law never intended the reasonable doubt standard of proof to be a shield, something for somebody to hide behind. No, sir. And that's what he, Mr. Meek, tried to do a while ago—use that standard to cloak her wrongdoing. And I know this. Y'all are too smart to fall for that. I know y'all will do the right thing, and that's find her guilty of these offenses your fellow citizens—your friends and neighbors and fellow workers—who comprised the grand jury charged her with. Speaking for my office and the members of your local law enforcement and on behalf of the People of this State and the law-abiding, God-fearing citizens of this community, I thank y'all." Parrish bowed and sat down.

***

The jury, which took less than time to agree upon a verdict than it took the judge to instruct them, found Ginger not guilty of both counts within the indictment as well as the lesser-included offense of grand larceny. When the clerk published the verdict, Ginger broke into tears, sobbing loudly. Even Dixie's eyes welled up.

As for Deloris, he scarce could believe what he had just heard, so convinced he was the jury's quick return indicated a guilty verdict. He had expected the worse, especially since the Tumbleton woman had lied on the witness stand and, in so doing, made it appear he had attempted to pull a fast one. Now, he found himself collapsed in his chair, his heart pounding so hard he feared it would burst through the wall of his chest at any moment. He had difficulty breathing and even seeing, his eyes being watered so.

The judge called for quiet in the courtroom and banged his gavel twice on top of his desk to achieve it. Most of the spectators, it seemed, approved of the verdict as there had been a scattering of applause when the clerk spoke the words "not guilty."

Parrish sat at his counsel table, his chin resting in the palm of his hand. Holcomb, wide-eyed and breathing hard, kept looking to his right and to his left, his mouth hanging open and his brow furrowed. He gave the appearance of one who had lost his way.

"Mr. Solicitor," the judge said, "there's one thing I want to resolve here and now, sir, if you don't mind."

Parrish struggled to his feet, his eyes directed to the floor. "Yes, sir?"

"I want the record to reflect, and I want you, Mr. Solicitor, to draft me an order to this effect." The judge read from notes on a legal pad, 'I find as a matter of law and of fact that the ventriloquist puppet or doll referred to as 'Kuddles' was abandoned on September 2, 1970, and as such was property open to possession and ownership by anyone who might seize it at that time and place. Inasmuch as Miss Ginger Childree, according to the evidence offered here, seized possession of the aforementioned abandoned property on the date at the time and place and under the circumstances as set forth in the record here, I find that she is now Kuddles' true and rightful owner.' " Judge Davis looked up from his notes and down at the solicitor. "Are you clear about what I want you to do, sir?"

"Yes, sir, Your Honor. I'll get it to you within a few minutes, sir. I'll get somebody in the clerk's office downstairs to type it up for me."

The judge motioned to Ginger. "Miss Childree, you may now take possession of the puppet from the court reporter. It now belongs to you, ma'am."

"But Judge," Holcomb cried out, "you can't do that?"

"Sir, what do you mean, I can't do that. I just did it. Say another word and I'll put you under the jail. You get me, sir?" The judge stood and parked his chair against the desk. "Court is recessed until nine thirty in the morning." He looked at Deloris. "Counsel, if you and Miss Childree can wait, the solicitor will have the order prepared for my signature in a jiffy."

Deloris could hardly speak so overcome was he by the turn of events. "Thank you, Your Honor," he said when he found his voice.

***

Deloris, Ginger, and Dixie left the courthouse by a side entrance. As the four walked along the sidewalk, someone yelled for Deloris to stop a moment. He turned and saw a man he recognized as one of the petit jurors hurrying toward him.

Deloris told his companions to walk on ahead, promising he'd meet them at his truck. He switched his brief case from one hand to the other as he waited on the juror.

"Mr. Meek," the man said, as he drew near all out of breath, "could I have a word with you, please sir?"

"Sure. And what's your name again, sir?"

"Hatcher. Gilbert Hatcher. Folks call me Gilly. I was on the jury. I sat on the back row."

"Yeah, I remember you. And thank you for what all y'all did. Y'all did the right thing, believe me."

Deloris looked at his watch. It was getting close to the time he usually drank him a beer or two. He and the women with him had planned to visit a tavern on the edge of town to celebrate Ginger's acquittal and her good fortune in regaining possession of Kuddles.

"So, what can I do for you, sir?"

Hatcher glanced all around. He appeared to swallow. "I'm sorry to bother you, but I wanted to tell you what went on in the jury room, if you got a minute. I thought maybe you might wanna know how we reached our verdict."

Deloris, his curiosity peaked, nodded. "Yeah, I sure would. Thank you."

"Remember the woman you put on the witness stand who said she didn't know Brother Holcomb?"

Deloris felt his heartbeat quicken. "Remember her? I'll never forget her. She perjured herself on the witness stand, and I got witnesses to prove she did."

"Yes, sir," the man said. "Well, anyway, and you tell me if I did anything wrong. She said she didn't do anything but attend a service and she didn't do an altar call the time she went out there to his tent." Hatcher looked all around. "Well, I knew for a fact she told a big ol' story."

"And how'd you know that, sir?"

"Cause I was there that night my ownself when she came to it—me and my wife were. She sat right there in front of us. She not only made an altar call, but before she did that, she went to the front and got on the stage with the preacher and the two of them commenced to dancing with each other like they could've been Ginger Rogers and Fred What-his-name. When it finally hit me she was the woman who'd done that, I didn't know what to do—whether to say anything about it or not. So, like my mama used to tell me, 'when in doubt, do nothing,' I kept my mouth shut. You know, the judge, he'd asked us before we got put on the jury whether we knew anything about the case or not. Well, at the time, I didn't know she was going to be a witness, and I sure didn't know she'd get up there on the witness stand and tell a big ol' story like she did."

"How'd you happen to remember her, Mr. Hatcher?"

"How, sir? Like I told you. She sat right there in front of me and my wife. And she's the type of woman who kinda stands out, sir—well dressed, big, real long brown hair, a ton of makeup on her face, and enough perfume on to float the Battleship Missouri. The main thing, though, is I well remember her when she was dancing on the stage, carrying on. I still have the mental picture of her and the preacher, the two of them on that stage, boogying around like a couple of teenagers in heat. I suppose what makes her stand out in my mind was that night at the tent she struck me as somebody who had too much religion—not too much Jesus, mind you, but too much religion.

"Anyhow, when we got back there in the jury room, I told everybody about what I'd seen. They asked me whether I was sure it was her, and I told them hell yeah I was sure, just as sure of that as I was of my name being Gilbert Hatcher. When I told them that, everybody agreed if the two of them would lie about not knowing one another, then the preacher had to be lying about what'd happened out there at the picnic grounds.

"So, Mr. Meek, that's how we arrived at our verdict. We never thought she took a shot at him. There wasn't any evidence she did. All the State presented was mere speculation, if even that. The main question we discussed had to do with the larceny count and whether she intended to steal the dummy when she put it in her car and took it on home with her. We all finally came to the conclusion we could see how, under the circumstances, she figured the preacher'd left it there on purpose for her to take back home with her. I can't tell you how happy it made us on the jury when the judge, later on, let her have the dummy for keeps. It made us feel like we'd done the right thing, you see."

Deloris stood facing the man in silence for a moment. "The thought'd crossed my mind, Mr. Hatcher, that maybe he intentionally left the dummy out there with the aim of incriminating Miss Childree—you know, getting back at her for suing him that time. I mean, his story about her shooting at him. Come on. That little woman wouldn't hurt a fly."

"Yes, sir, you could be right."

Before you go, Mr. Hatcher, there's one thing you might should do."

"Sir?"

"Me and my friends, we've just come from the judge's office. He's still there. He said he'd be there for a while. Said he had some other orders to sign and so forth. You might oughtta go tell him what you told me."

Hatcher's brow grew tight. "Really, Mr. Meek?" Hatcher's voice had a ring of uncertainty about it.

"Yes," Deloris answered with a nod.

"But what about me not saying nothing when the judge asked if anybody knew anything about the case?"

"Don't worry about it. You couldn't've known somebody you'd seen before only one time was going to be a witness. And anyway, merely hearing her name mentioned as a witness in the case wouldn't have meant anything to you since you didn't know her. Look at it like this, Mr. Hatcher. You did your duty. You lived up to your oath as a juror. You made sure the verdict spoke the truth."

Deloris took the man's hand and shook it. "I don't know what else to say, sir, other than thank you again."

"Funny thing, Mr. Meek."

"What's that?"

"I don't know what the jury would've decided about the larceny charge had the reverend and the Tumbleton woman told us the truth about knowing each other. Tell you something, though, when you questioned Kuddles about her voice change, I thought that was pretty durn clever of you."

Deloris clapped Hatcher on the back and ducked his head. "Thank you, Mr. Hatcher, but I have a confession to make. The idea to question Kuddles like that when Holcomb was operating her didn't come from me. It was Miss Childree's idea."

"Really? I'm not sure, though, it made any difference in the final outcome one way or the other, to be honest. Although I found

Kuddles' testimony very entertaining, I didn't know quite what to make of it. I know we didn't discuss it in the jury room. Wasn't any need to. I have to say, however, to suggest a demon had taken possession of the dummy was kinda stretching things, don't you think?

"But, at the same time, her testimony did illustrate, when Kuddles' operation by Brother Holcomb was contrasted with that by Miss Childree, how inappropriate Holcomb's possession of the dummy was. Speaking for myself only, it made me sympathetic toward Miss Childree and, for that matter, Kuddles. The situation reminded me—and I know this sounds silly—similar to one where a loving mother is wrongfully denied custody of her child. You could sense Kuddles and Miss Childree belonged together, making their relationship one worth her fighting for."

Deloris was at a loss of words. He said simply what was in his heart. "You're a good man, Mr. Hatcher."

Hatcher turned to walk away. He hesitated and spun back around. "Mr. Meek, please tell Miss Childree she belongs on TV."

CHAPTER ELEVEN

A month had passed when early on a frosty Tuesday morning Deloris sauntered into the Grease Pit for a hot breakfast of pork brains, eggs, and grits. A number of students from the college across the highway occupied round, Naugahyde-covered stools positioned around the counter. Glory Hiers, stood behind the counter by the cash register while her husband Rufus prepared the orders.

"Morning, Glory," Deloris said.

Glory looked up from a newspaper spread out before her atop the counter. "Oh, hey there, Deloris. You seen the paper this morning?"

"Not yet. Why?"

"You remember the woman you told me lied when you defended Ginger Childree up in Greenfield County?"

Deloris selected a stool and seated himself. "Yeah," he said, twisting toward her. "What about her?"

I read the other day where they'd arrested her for perjury. The tent preacher too, Dr. Holcomb, I believe his name was. You gonna represent one of them?"

"Naw, I only represent the innocent, doncha know."

"Well, you ain't gonna make no money thataway," Glory allowed.

Deloris pointed to the coffee maker. How about some of your coffee." As an afterthought he added, "And slide the paper this way, if you don't mind."

She pushed the newspaper over to him. "You want your usual?"

"Right-o. Thanks."

"Rufus," she yelled.

"Yeah, Glory?" her husband answered as he laid strips of bacon onto the grill. They sizzled almost immediately, blending their aroma with those emitted by the coffee maker, the toaster, and the grill.

"Deloris is here. Fix him his usual."

"Hey, there, Deloris," Rufus shouted. "You bought my Christmas present yet?"

Troubles and Kuddles

Glory's face grew angry. "Damn your sorry soul, Rufus, you mind what you're doing. I do the greeting around here, not you. How many times have I gotta tell you? And hell no, he ain't bought you no Chrtistmas present. I ain't either, and I ain't gonna buy you one. Get to work."

Rufus ignored his wife and returned to his job overseeing the grill.

Glory poured Deloris a cup of coffee and brought it to him. "Could I tell you something," she said, leaning toward him and placing her elbows on the countertop and looking straight at Deloris.

He continued to read. "Sure."

"Well, you gotta listen, if I'm gonna tell you."

Deloris looked up. "Okay, what?"

"A Yankee fella come in here late last night. After he got done eating his grilled cheese, he asked me if I happened to know you. I told him, of course I did. I said everybody—well, not everybody, but a lotta people knew you. He then asked me 'bout whether I knew Ginger and that Teal fella she does that brand-new TV show with on Channel 37. I said we couldn't get Channel 37 caused we didn't have no UHF antennae, but I knew who him and her were on account of you."

"You say he was a Yankee? Was he kinda stocky, not too tall, about forty years old, wore black and white shoes?"

"I didn't see what kinda shoes he had on, but the way you describe him sounds kinda like him all right."

"And all he wanted to know was whether you knew me and Ginger?"

"And the fella she partnered with." Glory leaned back and crossed her arms. "What's he want with y'all, honey? Any idea?"

"If it's who I think it was, he's an investigator for some bank, or at least he says he is. It has something to do with Wally's uncle." Deloris turned to the sports section in the paper. "He say anything else?"

"He said he'd gone yesterday afternoon to where you'd usually parked your truck at but said he didn't see it there. Said he went back by there a couple of more times and never did see it.

Said he'd been here in town a couple of months ago but had to hurry back north for a while, and he'd just got back to town and was wanting to talk to you. Said he'd had a death in his family, a brother, believe he said. He told me he had to help get the probate started and all and do some other things."

A student approached the cash register.

"Excuse me, Miss Deloris—Sir." Smiling, she took the young man's money and green order slip and stuck the latter on a small metal stalk next to the cash register. "Thank you, honey. Everything okay?"

"Yessum," he answered.

"Come back, now. And study real hard, make your mama and daddy proud, you hear?"

The student shook a toothpick from a bottle once used for green peppers and smiled. "Yes, ma'am, I will."

Glory returned to where Deloris sat. "I told the man the reason he didn't see your truck parked there no more was cause you now had you a brand-new office downtown. I told him where it was at." She stepped back, a concerned look on her face. "I hope I done the right thing, baby—you know, me telling him where he could find your law office at."

Deloris batted the air with his hand. "Sure it was. Who knows, he might be bringing me a wreck case involving a tractor-trailer."

***

Deloris parked his truck in the lot behind his office building. Shivering from the cold, he wasted no time in making for the back door. The moment he stepped into the hallway that lead to his private office he shed his overcoat. Just as he closed the door behind him, Dixie St. John appeared at the other end of the hallway.

"I thought I heard you pull in the driveway," she said. "You've got a customer. Can you see him now?"

"Sure," Deloris replied. "Send him on back."

Deloris waited in the hallway. A moment later, Jade Ziglar walked through the door, a hand extended in greeting.

Troubles and Kuddles

"Morning, counselor," Ziglar said, grinning as he swaggered toward Deloris. "This won't take long."

Deloris smiled. "Nice to see you," he lied. "I heard you were in town. They told me at Grease Pit you'd dropped by there last night." He pointed toward his opened door. "Come on in and take a seat."

Deloris followed the man inside.

"I heard you'd lost your brother," Deloris said. "I'm very sorry."

"Thank you. He'd been sick a long time. Parkinson's. In a way, it was kind of a blessing he died. His life had become hard on everybody, particularly on him."

"I can imagine." Deloris tilted back in his chair and steeped his hands. "So, what can I do for you, sir?"

"Last week the bank notified me the police had solved the murder of Fromberg's uncle. They arrested a known burglar, and he confessed to killing Mr. Goldmann. So, it would appear Eli Fromberg will be inheriting a sizeable estate after all."

Deloris sat drop-mouthed. "So, you drove or flew all the way here to tell me that?"

"And to find Fromberg. I've got some papers he needs to sign, if he doesn't want to return home and do everything there. Remember I told you Mr. Goldmann's will designated the bank to serve as the personal representative for his estate and they hired me to help them with the administration of the estate? That's all I'm doing. Trying to facilitate things for everybody concerned."

"I see." Deloris dropped his hands into his lap and scooted forward. "Where are you staying?"

"Here in town, at the Hotel Beauregard." Ziglar pulled a pack of cigarettes from his top left shirt pocket. He tapped a cigarette loose from a pack of Chesterfields and offered the pack to Deloris. "Care for one, Counselor."

Deloris declined the proffer.

Ziglar dug out a cigarette lighter and lit his cigarette. "Would you happen to know where I might find Fromberg?"

"Last contact I had with him and Ginger Childree, they were doing a TV show in Greenfield."

"Yeah, that's what the woman at the restaurant told me last night. But would you happen to know where he lives?"

"I suppose there in Greenfield. I don't keep up with him or with his partner, Ginger Chileree. You might try the TV station there this afternoon, Channel 37."

"Why this afternoon?"

"They do a kids show in the late afternoon weekdays. Doing quite well, from everything I hear."

Ziglar stood and stretched out his hand. "Thank you, counselor. I appreciate your help."

Deloris pushed back his chair, got to his feet, and took Ziglar's hand. "When you see them, give them both my best regards and tell them to call me sometime. I'd like to know how they're doing. Tell Wally—that is, Eli—I'm happy about his good fortune and all." He laughed. And also tell them both to stay outta trouble and avoid hecklers."

"Avoid hecklers?"

"They'll know what I mean."

***

Immediately after Deloris heard the front door slam shut Dixie appeared in the doorway of his office.

"What'd that slime ball want?" Dixie asked.

"Now why'd you call him a slime ball?"

"Because he is one." She waved her hand. "How could you stand being around him? He had on so much cologne it pure made my eyes water. Lord, if he and Maxine Tumbleton ever got together, people would keel over dead."

Deloris smiled. "To answer your question, he wanted to know where he might could find Wally. I told him Greenfield where they do their TV show. I suggested he drop by the station there."

"Should you have done that?"

"Why not? He told me Wally was no longer a suspect in his uncle's murder and would now inherit his estate. Doncha think Wally ought to know that? I'd sure wanna know if it was me."

"Me too, provided the guy was telling the truth."

"Why wouldn't he be?"

"Deloris, Deloris, Deloris, did you get a good look at him? Why, I wouldn't trust him if he held a license to preach and a lifetime notary commission. I bet if they ever hooked him up to a lie detector, the thing'd burst into flames after the first question."

"You don't know that."

"Betcha."

"Okay, I'll prove I can trust him," Deloris said after a moment of silence. "He told me he was staying at the Hotel Beauregard."

"Now why would he lie about where he was staying?"

"Well, all I'm saying is he told me something we can quickly check on to test his veracity."

"Deloris, sometimes, you're just plain weird."

"Look, Dixie, if he lied about where he was staying while he's here in town that'd mean he didn't want to leave a trail regarding where he's been."

"You come up with that all by yourself?"

Deloris ignored the put-down. He withdrew a telephone directory from a drawer to his desk and leafed through several pages.

"What number you looking up?" Dixie asked.

"The one for the Hotel Beauregard." He thumbed through the Yellow Pages. "Here tis."

He dialed the number for the hotel.

A voice on the other end of the phone answered, identifying the number called as the Hotel Beauregard.

"This is Deloris Meek. I'm a lawyer here in town, and I'm looking for a Mr. Jade Ziglar. I'm told he may be staying there. Could you tell me whether he's registered there by any chance?"

"Jade Ziglar, you say? Give me a minute, please." A silence followed. "Sir," said the voice, "we don't have anyone registered by that name."

Deloris bolted forward in his chair. "You don't? Well, did he check out already?"

A moment passed.

"Sir, we've not had a guest registered by that name—not for last night, sir, we haven't."

"You sure? He told me he was staying there."

"He could've been confused. But excuse me a minute. Let me look over at our registrations for the last week." A minute or two later, the voice returned to the phone. "Sir, no one by the name of Jade Ziglar or any name sounding like that has stayed with us within the last two weeks or so. Also, we don't have a reservation for anyone by that name."

Deloris thanked the hotel employee and hung up the phone. He gulped. "Dixie, I gotta get in touch with Wally. I hate to admit it, but Ziglar lied to me about staying at the Hotel Beauregard."

Dixie smirked. "See there. I told you he was a slime ball. Applying your little truth test, if he lied to you about his hotel, then you have to wonder what else he's lying about. Right?"

Deloris sighed. He hated it when Dixie got the best of him. "You're right. Will you try and get Wally for me?"

Dixie hurried from the room to return to her desk out front. Several minutes later she called Deloris on the intercom. "Deloris, I get no answer."

"In that case, Dixie, I better head for Greenfield."

"I'm going with you," Dixie said.

"But Dixie—"

"I said I'm going with you," Dixie said. "Meet you out back."

***

Deloris pulled into the Greenfield city limits. "Reckon we oughtta go by their apartment first?

"She doesn't still work at the bottling plant?" Dixie asked.

"No. She quit once she and Wally got their TV show going. You didn't answer my question. Should we see if they're at her apartment?"

Dixie shook her head. "I doubt if they'd be there. We didn't get any answer to our telephone call. If I had to guess, I'd say they're at the TV station. You know, rehearsing for their afternoon show. We might should go there first."

"Wherever it is," Deloris said. "If you see a phone booth, holler."

Troubles and Kuddles

They rode a few blocks further until Deloris spotted a booth outside a gas station a Pepsi sign advertised as "Buster's Oil and Gas and Tire Exchange." "There's one," he said. "See it?"

Dixie nodded as Deloris made a right turn into the station.

"I gotta get some gas anyway," Deloris said.

He glided his vehicle to a concrete island on which sat two gas tanks. An attendant in greasy overalls exited the station across from the red, white, and blue tanks, wiping his hands on a towel. He hurried to the driver side of Deloris' truck.

"I'll have the Ethyl. Fill'er up," Deloris said as he stepped from the truck and headed for the phone booth.

Fifteen minutes after leaving the gas station, Deloris pulled into the parking lot of the TV station. "I sure hope we find them inside," Deloris said as he cut the motor.

Deloris held the door for Dixie as they entered the television station. A receptionist sat at a desk several feet in front of entryway, reading a magazine. A television set, tuned to the station's channel, played to an arrangement of two chairs and a sofa, each one empty.

The attractive young woman looked up from her magazine and smiled. "May I help you?"

"Hi," Deloris said, also smiling. "I'm Deloris Meek, attorney at law, and this is my secretary Miss St. John. "Could you tell me if by any chance Ginger Childree might be here? I'm her lawyer, and I need to speak to her."

"You just missed her. She and Mr. Teal, they left here about ten minutes ago with another gentleman."

Deloris and Dixie looked at each other.

"Could you tell me what the other man looked like, Miss?"

"To be honest, I didn't pay much attention to him. About the only thing I noticed about him was he wore black and white shoes and had a northern accent."

"Ziglar!" Deloris declared. "Did they say where they were headed?"

"No, sir. But if you want me to, I can call back and ask their director to see if he might know."

"If you will, please, ma'am. And thank you".

The receptionist dialed a number and spoke to someone on the other end of the phone. "Thank you," she said as she ended their conversation. "Mr. Meek, Mr. Strickland—he's our program director—he said he hadn't noticed they'd left. He said he's been busy reviewing some program logs. He thinks maybe they went out to get them something to drink. They sometimes'll do that. He said they'd probably be back in few minutes." She nodded toward the TV set. "If you care to wait."

"I don't think we have any choice, Dixie, but to sit and wait a while to see if they come back," Deloris said.

"And if they don't?"

"I dunno."

Thirty minutes passed without Ginger and Wally returning to the television station. Deloris looked at his watch. "Dixie, their show's supposed to go on the air at five, and here it is a quarter after four. I hope they're ready and don't have to rehearse anymore."

"I guess they know what they're doing, Deloris. A lot of what they do is adlibbed anyway. You know, with the children and all and talking back and forth with them. There's no way of telling what those kids might say, and that's what makes their show entertaining, in my opinion."

"Speaking of children," Deloris said, angling his head toward the front door.

Several children, herded by two adults, came running into the station, laughing and talking notwithstanding the adults' efforts to hush and corralled them. Two children, both boys, raced over to the waiting area, pushing and shoving each other. One reached for the channel selector and twirled it around and around while the other boy climbed onto the sofa and used it as a trampoline. An adult hurried over and seized both children by the hand, admonishing them. She apologized to Deloris and Dixie as she led them away.

Dixie switched the channel back to the proper one. "Lord have mercy, "those two could serve as poster boys for birth control," she remarked as the woman ushered her charges through a door to the receptionist's left.

Troubles and Kuddles

Deloris surmised the door led to the studio in which Ginger's and Wally's show originated.

More minutes ticked away, and still no Ginger and Wally.

"Reckon something's happened to them, Dixie? I'm getting a little worried about them."

Before she could answer, Ginger walked through the door. She spotted Deloris the moment she entered the reception area. "Deloris. Dixie. How nice to see you."

"Wally's not with you?" Deloris asked.

"Nope. I'm afraid I'll have to do the show all by myself this afternoon and most likely for the next several days."

Deloris and Dixie exchanged concerned looks.

"Yeah?" Deloris said.

"Yes. Wally just found out he's come into some money. He's got to return to New Jersey and meet with the probate court. You know legal stuff. It was all over my head." She smiled. "What are y'all doing here?"

"When is he leaving Greenfield?"

"When? Soon as he can go by our apartment and pack him a few things. He's going to ride back with Mr. Ziglar."

"Is that the same apartment you lived in when I represented you?"

"Yes. Why?"

Deloris motioned to Dixie. "Come on. Maybe we can catch them before they can leave."

"Is something wrong, Mr. Meek?" Ginger asked.

"I don't have time to explain it to you right now," Deloris said, speaking fast. "How about doing this for us—call your apartment and tell Wally not to leave until we've had a chance to speak to him."

Deloris took Dixie by the elbow and hurried her out the door. "We need to look for an out-of-state, black Cadillac with whitewall tires."

What should have been a ten-minute trip to Ginger's apartment took Deloris a little more than fifteen minutes. Almost every traffic light he encountered required him to stop and the drivers of the motor vehicles ahead of him on the streets drove as if they suffered from sleeping sickness.

As he rounded the corner onto the street where Ginger's apartment building stood, Deloris swore to himself. He saw no black Cadillac. "I'm afraid, Dixie," he said, as he pulled in a loading zone in front of Ginger's apartment building and stopped, "we've missed them."

"I'll tell you what I believe we should do," she said.

"What?"

"Do you know which highway they're likely to take to drive from Greenfield to New Jersey?"

Deloris thought a few seconds. He nodded. "There's not but one. Highway 711."

"Take it," she said.

"Take it? You mean, follow them?"

"Why sure. You've got a tank full of gas. Maybe we can catch them before you need to stop again for another fill-up. What other choice have we got?"

"None, I don't reckon."

Deloris put the truck in first gear and, looking into the side mirror, re-entered the street. "Holler if you see a Cadillac with New Jersey plates on it."

***

Deloris glimpsed his speedometer. "Dixie, we've gone about thirty miles. If Ziglar's driving fast, we'll never overtake him. I'm going as fast as this thing can go. It's not built for speed but for practicing law, you know."

Dixie harrumphed. "It wasn't even built for that. It was built for milk delivery, for goodness sake. Besides, I thought you told me you'd souped it up so you could chase after ambulances."

"I never said any such thing."

A combination filling station and restaurant came into view as Deloris topped a hill along both sides of which stood towering rows of pine trees.

Dixie pointed toward the station. "Why don't we stop yonder? I could use me something to eat. And I wouldn't mind using the restroom either."

"Oh, don't tell me you've again got a bladder problem. Please don't tell me that. I remember the last time you—"

"No, I don't, but I still would like to have some crackers or something. Aren't you a little hungry?"

Deloris nodded. "I suppose so."

As Deloris approached the station, Dixie exclaimed, "Deloris! Look yonder!"

"What?" he said.

"There in the parking lot. That black car. Isn't it a Cadillac?"

Deloris slowed down and directed his sight to the parking lot a short distance ahead and the car in question. It sat by itself, yards from the nearest motor vehicle and far removed from any station facility. "Yeah, I believe it is, by George." He redirected his eyes to the road. "You see anybody in it?"

"No. It's my guess they're inside. Tell you what. Let me out while you go park. I'll run inside to see."

"But what if Ziglar sees you."

"I'll try not to be noticed."

Deloris grunted. "Now that's damn near impossible, Dixie."

"So what if he does see me? He won't know we were chasing them. He'll think our meeting them is nothing more than a coincidence. Why wouldn't he? I'll tell him we've been to a court hearing. How's that?"

Dixie stepped from the truck. Before she shut the door, she turned around. "How about handing me my purse."

Deloris lifted her purse from off the floorboard. "My goodness, Dixie, what in the world do you have in here, anvils?"

"Just hand it to me. I don't need any of your smart comments."

As Dixie hurried inside the building, Deloris pulled into a parking space several yards from the Cadillac. Less than ten minutes later, Dixie appeared at Deloris' driver window.

"Well?"

Dixie giggled. "It's him, all right."

"How about Wally? See him?"

"Nope."

"You didn't?"

"And I waited a few minutes, too, to see if maybe he'd gone to the men's room."

"Did he see you?"

"No, his back was to me the whole time. He was too busy stuffing his mouth."

"That's funny. You know, Wally not being with him." Deloris stroked his chin. "Wonder what Ziglar'd say if he saw me?"

"You won't know unless you give him the chance. But if you'll excuse me, I've gotta run to the little girl's room."

Deloris exited the truck as Dixie, her right shoulder drooping from the weight of her handbag, hurried toward the women's restroom on the side of the building. He moseyed toward the Cadillac, his eye fixed on the front door of the restaurant. Upon nearing the automobile, he thought he heard a muffled sound coming from inside the trunk of the car. He paused and listened. He again heard the sound. He thought it sounded like someone moaning.

Deloris eased over to the rear of the car and tapped on the trunk lid. "Hello. Is anybody in there?"

Again, the moaning sound.

"Wally, if that's you, make that sound again."

Deloris heard the sound once more.

"I don't know how I can get you outta there, not without a key, I don't. Stay calm. I'm gonna go run call the police. They'll get you out."

Deloris heard more moaning, but this time it was louder and seemed more distressed.

As Deloris turned around, he spotted Ziglar walk through front door of the restaurant. He came to a halt and looked Deloris' way. Ziglar headed toward him, walking almost running.

"Hi there, Meek, whatcha doing here?" he said, upon reaching him and looking toward his car.

Ziglar inserted a hand inside his coat.

"Hey, Mr. Ziglar. Surprised to see you."

"Yeah, likewise."

"Thought I'd go in there and get me something to eat."

"Yeah?"

Ziglar stood facing Deloris, his back to the building, his right hand still inside his coat.

"How about you?" Deloris said. "You stop to eat?"

"Yeah. To eat. Wouldn't recommend it."

Deloris looked past Ziglar, hoping to see Dixie. He did not. *What a time for her to primp*, he thought. He smiled at Ziglar. "You ever get to talk to Fromberg?"

At the mention of Wally's real name, Deloris again heard the sounds he had heard minutes before.

Ziglar withdrew a revolver from inside his coat, stuck it into his right-coat pocket, and pointed it at Deloris. "All right, counselor, don't you try anything cute, and keep your hands where I can see them." He tilted his head toward the rear of the car. "I'm afraid I'm gonna have to let you ride back there with my little buddy. Might be a little uncomfortable for you, but it'll only be for a little while."

Ziglar waved the pistol at Deloris as Ziglar withdrew a set of car keys from inside his pants pocket with his free hand. "Here, catch," he said, tossing them to Deloris.

Deloris missed the throw, and the keys fell to the ground.

"Pick those up and pop the trunk open." Ziglar took a quick look around. "And hurry."

Deloris retrieved the keys and fiddled with them. "Which one's the trunk's?"

Ziglar raised his gun a bit higher. "Don't play stupid with me. Open the trunk, or I'll blow a hole in you so wide I could drive my car through it."

Deloris held up one of the keys on the key ring. "I'm guessing it's this one," Deloris said, attempting to stall. "Am I right?"

"I'm not going to tell you again. Open the damn trunk and do it now."

Deloris did as ordered. When he raised the trunk lid, he saw Wally scrunched up on the floor with both his feet and hands bound with electrical tape and his mouth gagged.

Suddenly, everything went black.

***

Deloris opened his eyes to find himself lying flat on his back. It was as though he had awakened from a deep sleep. He felt remarkably refreshed. Seconds later, however, a numbing pain in the back of his head made itself known as did something wet and sticky on his head and neck. He ran his fingers over his neck and through his hair. When he brought his hand around, he realized the wet and sticky something was blood—his own.

As he stared upwards, the face of an angel came into view and closed within inches of his. The face belonged to Dixie St. John. Behind her stood Root and Cab Johnson, their yellow-stained teeth exposed by their wide grins.

"Hey there, big fella," she said sweetly.

"What happened, Dixie?"

It all came back to him. He remembered standing in front of a car trunk and seeing Wally Teal on the trunk floor. And he remembered Jade Ziglar holding a gun on him and ordering him to climb into the trunk.

"When I came out of the restroom, I saw Ziglar hit you in the back of the head with his pistol and you fell forward into the trunk. That's when I snucked up behind him and let him have it with my purse. I swung it around with both my hands and hit him as hard as I could. I mean I let him have it right against the side of his head, knocking him onto the ground. Whenever I hit him, the gun scooted out of his hand. I ran over to grab it, but these two came running and beat me to it."

"Yes, sir," Root said. "We was here waitin' for the man I been cuttin' pulpwood for to come by and pay us when me and Cab, we seen what was happenin'."

Dixie continued. "And when he tried to get up, one of them—"

"It was me what done it, Lawyer Meek," Cab said.

"Yes, him," Dixie said. "He pointed the gun at Ziglar and told him to stay put. That's when the boy who pumps the gas came running over, as did several other people—customers, they looked like. Somebody called the sheriff. A couple of deputies are here now, talking to Wally and the attendant."

"They done talked to us too," Root said. His chest swelled. "They said we might be witnesses for the State. How 'bout that? Me and Cab being witnesses for the State. Mama'd be so proud."

"God bless her soul," Cab said, bowing his head.

Root looked toward the sky. "Mama, she always told us we wouldn't never 'mount to nothin' and now look at us. We gonna be state witnesses. Both of us."

"How about Ziglar? Where's he?" Deloris asked.

"Under arrest," Dixie said. She pointed to the squad car parked beneath the awning. He's sitting in that car yonder."

"And you hit him with your purse?"

"What else? Didn't you say you thought I carried anvils around in it?"

Dixie helped Deloris to his feet a moment before a long, black motor vehicle drove into the station lot, its siren wailing. Two men jumped out and ran forward as the sound of the siren faded. One carried a medical bag.

"Good," Dixie said. "They're from the funeral home."

"The funeral home? But I ain't dead, Dixie."

"I know that, silly. They're here to give you first aid and get you to the hospital." She scowled. "You know sometime, Deloris, you can be just plain goofy."

As the ambulance attendants loaded Deloris into the ambulance, Root, who had opened the door for them, looked at Deloris on the stretcher and said. "Wanna hear some good news, Lawyer Meek? Lawyer Chiselbrook, he settled our watermelon case with the Nickel Jamboree and for three hundred dollars. Sure did. Me and Cab, after lawyer fees, court cost, . . ."

"Notary fee," Cab said.

"Notary fee? For what?" Deloris said.

"Lawyer Chiselbrook charged it on count the papers me and Cab signed. they had to be—what's the word he used?—'very fried.' "

"You mean 'verified,' " Deloris said. "Root, are you telling me he charged y'all for notarizing the verification on the complaint he served on y'all's behalf?"

"He said it was the law," Root said. "And we had to pay a courthouse entry fee, but it wasn't too much, only three dollar each. He told us it'd been five-dollar iffen we'd gone to trial, so he saved us two dollar each by settlin' the case."

"He charged us a lawyer tax, too. Don't forget it," Cab said.

"Lawyer tax?" Deloris asked.

"Yes, sir," Root said. "After paying it, which Lawyer Chiselbrook said was a hundred dollar, and payin' all them other charges, me and Cab, we cleared eighty-seven dollar and thirteen-cent. You gotta admit that's pretty good for a thirty-five-cent watermelon, now ain't it?"

CHAPTER TWELVE

Shortly before noon, Deloris, fresh from the hospital where he had stayed overnight, hung up the telephone after talking to Assistant Attorney General Billy Joe Pratt. He had called Deloris to check on his condition and update him on a recent development regarding Jade Ziglar.

Moments later, Dixie, Ginger, and Wally walked into Deloris' office and arrayed themselves in chairs placed around the front of his desk. The latter carried two large, black cases. They set them at their feet.

Deloris greeted the three. He turned around in his swivel chair, exposing the back of his head. "Tell me the truth, Dixie," he said, "this place on the back of my head where they shaved and stitched it up, does it look real funny to you?"

Dixie stood and took a close look. "You're sure you wanna know the truth?"

"Sure, I do. I wouldn't've asked you if I didn't."

"No. It doesn't look funny."

Deloris sighed in relief as he turned back around. "It doesn't?"

"No, it doesn't. It looks hilarious. It's a regular thigh slapper." She giggled. "Don't y'all think so, Ginger? Wally?"

Both agreed with Dixie and laughed.

Deloris dropped his chin onto his chest. Wonder how long it'll take for my hair to grow back?"

"Six or seven months, I'd say," Wally said with a wink. "Assuming it will grow at all."

"I agree," Dixie said.

"Oh, me," Deloris said, resignation evident in his voice. He tilted his head to the side. "Let me ask y'all something. Why y'all here, Wally—you and Ginger?"

"Why? We heard from the sheriff's office. They've had a chance to interview Ziglar, and he gave them a full, signed confession."

Deloris grunted. "As if one was needed. He was caught red-handed with you, Wally, in the trunk of his car, bound and gagged. Then there's Dixie's seeing him attack me, and her and the Johnson boys rescuing me."

"That's true. His confession had more to do with why he had kidnapped me than what he did to you."

"Oh." His tone seemed one of disappointment.

"It pretty much all had to do with my uncle's estate. His last will and testament left everything to me. But, there was a catch. He didn't want the gift to vest in me until the time of distribution, that is, until after all the obligations of his estate had been satisfied. Why he wanted to do it that way, I don't know. Maybe he didn't know what the extent of his debts would be when he died or maybe he preferred his grandnephew over my heirs. In any case, under his will, if I were to die before the distribution, everything would go to a grand nephew, Edward Dentz, and not to any of my designees or heirs."

"But I thought Ziglar told me there wasn't any residuary clause."

"He lied to you."

Goldmann's will expressly named Dentz as an alternative heir and legatee. Long story short, Dentz hired Ziglar to—you know—make sure I wouldn't make it to 'distribution time,' if I may phrase it like that."

"Why didn't Ziglar try to kidnap and kill Wally earlier, I wonder?" Dixie said.

"This is what the investigating officers told me. Ziglar and the nephew thought I had killed my uncle, and had such been the case, the law would have prohibited me from inheriting anything from him. So, there would've been no need for them to kill me and risk being caught and sentenced to the electric chair. But once Ziglar and the grandnephew learned a burglar had confessed to the murder, their plans changed. They had to kill me for Dentz to inherit Uncle Izzy's property."

"What delayed the distribution?" Deloris asked.

"Denz himself caused a lot of the holdup, as it turns out. Under an assumed name, he signed a contract to purchase my uncle's home and used it to delay the closing for several months, claiming the roof leaked and needed to be repaired or there was some mold in the basement. Stuff like that."

"Let me ask you this, if you know," Deloris said. "Did Ziglar's brother really have Parkinson's and was that why we didn't have any kind of contact with him for a while?"

Wally shook his head. "The officers told me it was all a lie. Ziglar told you what he did, Mr. Meek, to account for the interruption in his so-called investigation. Again, once the burglar confessed to my uncle's murder, they decided to put Plan B into operation."

Deloris rubbed his mouth. "Changing the subject, Wally, the sheriff's been in contact with the New Jersey authorities, and Ziglar has agreed to waive extradition to New Jersey where he and Uncle Izzy's grandnephew will answer to charges of conspiracy to commit murder. Later on, New Jersey will send Ziglar back down here to Greenfield County to be tried for assaulting you and me and kidnapping you."

"Is that right?" Wall responded.

"Yeah. Right before y'all came in, Billy Joe Pratt called me from the attorney general's office and told me about him waiving extradition. Billy Joe handles all the extradition requests for the State. He's been in touch with the New Jersey folks to kinda speed this thing along, he told me."

"I'm not surprised Ziglar'd waive extradition," Wally said. "I understand, during his interrogation, he told them if he had to serve time he, to use his words, 'sure as hell didn't want to serve it down here.' "

After several more minutes of conversation, Wally and Ginger stood to leave. Deloris came around from behind his desk. Ginger hugged both Deloris and Dixie. Wally also hugged Dixie, kissing her on the cheek as he did so. He turned from Dixie and extended a hand to Deloris while placing his other on Deloris' shoulder.

"I'll never forget you two folks, Mr. Meek. Never. I don't have the words to express to you and Miss St. John about how grateful I am to you both for saving my life. Looking back, it was a fateful day the day you gave Ginger and me a lift when were hitchhiking that time. If you had not come along, I'd be dead right now. The investigators told me he intended to kill me when he reached Lake Cureton. He planned to drown me and wanted my body found so there wouldn't be any holdups on the distribution of my uncle's estate."

Deloris smiled. "Keep in touch, Wally. And you too, Ginger. Good luck to both of you on your career."

Before I go, Mr. Meek, I'm curious about one thing," Wally said. "Why did Holcomb try to set Ginger up? We never did hear."

"I really don't know. He's never said. My investigator, Sergeant Unthank, thinks Holcome'd heard somebody—probably whoever it was who told him Ginger was working at the bottling plant—heard them say she had come to Awenasa. He probably figured she was following him and would make another go at getting Kuddles back. He might've wanted to put an end to her dogging him about Kuddles, and what better way to do that than have her locked up in jail for a good long while."

"Now, he'll be the one who'll be locked up," Ginger said quietly. "Kuddles' revenge, I call it."

Wally and Ginger also smiled at each other and nodded.

"One other thing," Ginger said, opening one of the black cases as Wally opened the other. "We each have something we want to show the two of you."

Ginger pulled a female dummy with a beautiful face and long blonde hair from her case. She inserted her hand into the back.

The dummy's head turned and faced Dixie. "Hey there. What is your name?" the dummy appeared to say.

Dixie laughed. "Dixie. And yours?"

"It's Dixie too. And I got peroxided hair, just like you and my cousin Kuddles have got."

"I see you do," Dixie said.

Wally pulled a male, pear-shaped dummy from his case. "And my name is Deloris. I spelled it with an 'i,' " the puppet appeared to say.

Everyone laughed.

ABOUT THE AUTHOR

BERT GOOLSBY, raised in Dothan, Alabama, is a retired appellate judge of the South Carolina Court of Appeals and a former Chief Deputy Attorney General of South Carolina. He attended the University of Alabama for one year prior to his entry into the U.S. Army. Following his honorable discharge from military service, he attended The Citadel where he received his B.A. degree and, after that, he attended the University of South Carolina School of Law, receiving his LL.B. degree. He later earned an LL.M degree at the University of Virginia. Among other publications, he has authored seven novels, two devotionals, and one law book. He and his wife, the former Mary Ellen "Prue" Fraser of Walterboro, South Carolina, make their home in Columbia, South Carolina. They have one son, Philip Lane Goolsby, M.D. of De Pere, Wisconsin.

www.ingramcontent.com/pod-product-compliance
Lightning Source LLC
Chambersburg PA
CBHW071533220526
45469CB00003B/754